Books for Cooks

number s[...]

by

Eric Treuillé
Jennifer Joyce
Ursula Ferrigno
Celia Brooks Brown

Decorated by Selina Snow 2005

PRYOR PUBLICATIONS
WHITSTABLE AND WALSALL
Specialist in Facsimile Reproductions
MEMBER OF
INDEPENDENT PUBLISHERS GUILD

75 Dargate Road, Yorkletts, Whitstable,
Kent CT5 3AE, England
Tel. & Fax (01227) 274655
E-mail: alan@pryor-publications.co.uk
www.pryor-publications.co.uk
Kent Exporter of the Year Awards
Shortlisted
International Business Awards
A full list of publications sent free on request.

© BOOKS FOR COOKS December 2005
ISBN 1- 905253-10-9
Cover by Selina Snow
Compiled by Rosie Kindersley
Published by Pryor Publications
For
BOOKS FOR COOKS
Tel: 0207 221 1992
Fax: 0207 221 1517
E-mail: info@booksforcooks.com
Website: www.booksforcooks.com

Printed and bound by
Estudios Graficos ZURE, S.A.
48950 – Erandio (Spain)

Reprinted February 2007

CONTENTS

THE BOOKS FOR COOKS COOKS

ERIC TREUILLÉ was born in Cahors in South West France. At the age of thirteen he was apprenticed as a charcutier; he went on to complete his culinary studies in Paris. Work as a restaurant chef took him from Paris to London, where he began a new career working as a food stylist with Anne Willan and Le Cordon Bleu cooking school. He discovered Books for Cooks, his wife Rosie Kindersley and a whole new career as combined cookery teacher, food writer and bookseller all on one fateful day in June 1993 when he crossed the threshold of 4 Blenheim Crescent.

JENNIFER JOYCE is a self-taught cook from the States. Her love of food began early while cooking for an Italian family of eleven! Until the birth of her first son Liam (since followed by a second, Riley) Jennifer was one of the mainstays of the Test Kitchen. She now concentrates on food writing and teaching. Her workshops focus on New American cooking – especially Southwestern, Fusion and Californian - and unusual ingredients and big bold flavours are very much the trademark of her classes.

URSULA FERRIGNO grew up on her father's vegetable and olive producing farm in southern Italy where she was taught to cook by her grandmother. She discovered Books for Cooks in 1991, when we were recommended as an ideal location for her popular Italian Day cookery demonstrations. She is the busiest person we know! In between writing a steady stream of wonderful cookbooks, she finds time to teach workshops at Books for Cooks and give cookery classes at cooking schools both in Italy and up and down the British Isles.

American-born CELIA BROOKS BROWN says that the very first day she walked into Books for Cooks she realised she'd arrived in a cook's paradise. She asked for a job at once! She began selling books in the shop but couldn't keep out of the kitchen for long, where her inspired and eclectic style of vegetarian cookery soon made its mark.

TOM KIME cut his culinary teeth at the River Café and with Rick Stein at Padstow before moving to Sydney to work at Darley Street Thai with David Thompson. It was while working with David that he learnt the refined traditions of Royal Thai cuisine - an experience that set him off on an on-going exploration of authentic Asian flavours. Today he divides his time between teaching, food consultancy, food writing and his own restaurant Food@The Muse just up the road from Books for Cooks.

It was the shock of English boarding school in the early 70's that convinced Japanese born KIMIKO BARBER that learning to cook was the necessity for survival. She first appeared at the Books for Cooks as a customer and an enthusiastic student of the workshop where (she says) she learnt the grammar of cooking from Eric. Fuelled by love of cooking and curiosity to broaden her culinary horizon, it wasn't long before she began a regular stint in the test kitchen and progressed to teaching Japanese and other Asian classes upstairs in the workshop kitchen. She is now divides her time between teaching and food writing.

JENNY CHANDLER travelled for over a decade, first with a backpack, and then cooking on yachts all over the world. She is passionate about food and travel and many of her recipes and ideas are gathered from her years on the move. She is now firmly rooted in Bristol where she runs her own cookery school, The Plum Cooking Company. The rest of her time is spent in Spain where she is currently researching a book on Spanish food festivals - a good excuse to live it up at all the local fiestas! Then, of course, there are frequent visits to Books for Cooks where she demonstrates mainly Spanish, North African and Southern Mediterranean food.

BLANCA VALENCIA credits her parents with her early interest in all things culinary. Adventurous travellers and eaters, they encouraged her to try everything at least once. A childhood divided between Spain and Latin America plus travels further afield ensured plenty of opportunities to fall in love with flavour. Eating and reading about food were, she says, her primary passions and, by the time she left college in the States to return to Madrid, she had a considerable collection of cookbooks. Back in Spain, she began cooking in earnest until work and a wedding took her to London. Finally she took the plunge, jacked in the highly-paid-and-pressured job and enrolled at cookery school. Le Cordon Bleu led her to the kitchen shop and cooking school round the corner, then Divertimenti led her, inexorably, we like to think, to Books for Cooks, through the good offices of Celia, who recommended her as an ideal candidate for Test Kitchen cook, which she has indeed proved to be!

MARILOU AMANTE is our kitchen assistant - and we couldn't do without her! Although she can turn her hand to most things in the kitchen, she especially enjoys baking, but at home she still cooks the traditional dishes of her native Philippines.

COOK BOOKS BY THE BOOKS FOR COOKS COOKS...

Favourite Recipes From Books for Cooks 1, 2 & 3 Victoria Blashford Snell, Jennifer Joyce, Eric Treuillé, Ursula Ferrigno, Sophie Braimbridge & Celia Brooks Brown (2001 Pryor Publications)

Favourite Recipes From Books for Cooks 4, 5 & 6 Eric Treuillé, Victoria Blashford Snell, Jennifer Joyce, Olivia Greco, Ursula Ferrigno, & Celia Brooks Brown (2005 Pryor Publications)

Canapés Eric Treuillé & Victoria Blashford Snell (1999 Dorling Kindersley)

Cordon Bleu Complete Cooking Techniques Eric Treuillé (1996 Cassell Illustrated)

Bread Eric Treuillé & Ursula Ferrigno (1999 Dorling Kindersley)

Barbecue Eric Treuillé & Birgit Erath (2000 Dorling Kindersley)

Pasta Eric Treuillé & Anna Del Conte (2000 Dorling Kindersley)

Diva Cooking Jennifer Joyce & Victoria Blashford Snell (2001 Mitchell Beazley)

The Well-Dressed Salad Jennifer Joyce (2004 Pavilion Books)

Lunch Boxes Jennifer Joyce (2005 Michael Joseph)

Small Bites Jennifer Joyce (2005 Dorling Kindersley)

Truly Italian Ursula Ferrigno (1999 Mitchell Beazley)

Risotto Ursula Ferrigno (2001 Ryland Peters and Small)

Bringing Italy Home Ursula Ferrigno (2001 Mitchell Beazley)

Real Fast Vegetarian Food Ursula Ferrigno (2002 Metro Books)

Truly Madly Pasta Ursula Ferrigno (2003 Quadrille Publications)

Italy Sea to Sky Ursula Ferrigno (2003 Mitchell Beazley)

Trattoria Ursula Ferrigno (2004 Mitchell Beazley)

Easy Italian Ursula Ferrigno (2005 Quadrille)

La Dolce Vita Ursula Ferrigno (2005 Mitchell Beazley)

Vegetarian Foodscape Celia Brooks Brown (1998 Pen and Ink)

New Vegetarian Celia Brooks Brown (2001 Ryland Peters and Small)

New Kitchen Garden Celia Brooks Brown with Adam Caplan (2003 Ryland, Peters and Small)

Entertaining Vegetarians Celia Brooks Brown (2003 Pavilion Books)

Low-Carb Vegetarian Celia Brooks Brown (2004 Pavilion Books)

World Vegetarian Classics Celia Brooks Brown (2005 Pavilion Books)

Sushi - Taste & Technique Kimiko Barber & Hiroki Takemura (2002 Dorling Kindersley)

Easy Noodles Kimiko Barber (2003 Ryland Peters & Small)

The Japanese Kitchen Kimiko Barber (2004 Kyle Cathie)

Exploring Taste + Flavour Tom Kime (2005 Kyle Cathie)

The Food of Northern Spain The Jenny Chandler (2005 Pavilion Books)

...AND SOME OF THEIR FAVOURITE COOKBOOKS

Avoca Café Cookbook 2 Hugo Arnold & Leylie Hayes (2002 Avoca Handweavers)
Café@Home Julie Le Clerc (2003 Penguin Books)
Casa Moro Sam & Sam Clark (2004 Ebury Press)
Cooking To Impress Without Stress Annabel Langbein (2003 Graphic Arts Centre)
India with Passion Manju Malhi (2004 Mitchell Beazley)
Just Like Mother Used To Make Tom Norrington Davies (2003 Cassell Illustrated)
Just One Pot Lindsey Bareham (2004 Cassell Illustrated)
Mary Berry's Ultimate Cake Book Mary Berry (2003 BBC Books)
River Café Cook Book Easy Rose Gray & Ruth Rogers (2003 Ebury Press)
The River Cottage Year Hugh Fearnley Whittingstall (2003 Hodder & Stoughton)
The River Cottage Meat Book Hugh Fearnley Whittingstall (2004 Hodder & Stoughton)
Sausage & Mash Fiona Beckett (2004 Absolute Press)
The Slow Mediterranean Kitchen Paula Wolfert (2003 John Wiley)
Soup Pippa Cuthbert & Lindsay Cameron Wilson (2006 New Holland)
Stylish Indian in Minutes Monisha Bharadwaj (2002 Kyle Cathie)
Tamarind & Saffron Claudia Roden (2000 Penguin Books)
A World In My Kitchen, Peter Gordon (2003 Hodder Moa Beckett)
Zarbo Mark McDonough (2002 Random House)
More Recipes from Zarbo Mark McDonough (2002 Random House)

PLEASE NOTE! For any out of print cookbooks, we thoroughly recommend that you contact -

Liz Seeber
www.lizseeberbooks.co.uk

NOTES ON THE RECIPES

BEFORE YOU COOK read through the recipe carefully. Make sure you have all the equipment and ingredients required.

ACCURATE MEASUREMENTS are essential if you want consistently good results each time. Always stick to one set of measurements, whether, imperial, metric or American cups, and never mix and match.

PREHEAT YOUR OVEN for 10-20 minutes before you need to use it. Bear in mind that the higher the temperature required, the longer it will take to preheat the oven.

OVENS DO VARY from kitchen to kitchen - so it's most worthwhile getting to know your own! Most have hot spots, so be prepared to rotate dishes from top to bottom or from front to back during cooking time. A good oven thermometer is invaluable! If using a fan-assisted oven, do follow the instructions for adjusting cooking timings and temperatures.

FRUIT AND VEGETABLES should be washed, trimmed and, unless otherwise stated in the recipe's ingredients list, peeled.

ALWAYS TASTE FOOD as you cook and before you serve. Ingredients differ from day to day, season to season, kitchen to kitchen. Be prepared to adjust sweetness, sharpness, spiciness, and, most important of all, salt, to your own taste.

BUY THE BEST you can afford. Whatever your cooking skills, the end result can only be as good as the ingredients you put in. Now that the Farmers' Market movement is beginning to grow in Britain, we should all soon have the opportunity to buy food that is not only seasonal but also produced locally and on a smaller scale. Call The National Association of Farmers' Markets on 01225 787914 or see their website www.farmersmarkets.net

EGGS ARE ORGANIC because, unless you know the supplier, the term free-range generally has little or no meaning. By organic we mean Soil Association Certified, because all other standards (including, at the time of writing, even the RSPCA Freedom Foods label) allow the unacceptably cruel practice of de-beaking.

LET US KNOW if you can't get a recipe to work. Please call us (even if you are in the middle of cooking a recipe!) so that we can help. Despite triple testing, mistakes do creep in, usually at the computer stage, we're afraid. Corrections can then be included in the next print run. Thank you!

Soups

SPICY SAUSAGE & WHITE BEAN SOUP
WITH ROAST CHERRY TOMATOES

This heartily flavoured and textured soup from our very own Tom Kime's inspirational first cookbook *Exploring Taste + Flavour* is also excellent when made with chorizo sausage. We use the Chicken, honey and herb sausages devised by Eric for Rosie's family farm Sheepdrove Organic Farm (see their website www.sheepdrove.com), but any really good pure meat (yes, that means no rusk, rice flour or other such sawdust) sausage will do.

Tom uses cannellini beans, but we rather favour butter beans, though you can use any bean you fancy.

SERVES 4

250 g (8 oz) cherry tomatoes, halved
4 tbsp olive oil
salt, black pepper
1 onion, finely chopped
200 g (7 oz) organic chicken or best pure meat sausages, skinned and
     roughly crumbled
4 garlic cloves, finely chopped
$1/4$ tsp crushed chilli flakes
1 – 400 g (14 oz) tin cannellini beans, drained and rinsed
750 ml (1 $1/4$ pints/3 cups) chicken or vegetable stock
1 tbsp balsamic vinegar
1 handful fresh flat-leaf parsley or basil leaves or a mixture
more olive oil to serve

HEAT THE OVEN to 180 C (350 F) Gas 4. Place the tomatoes in a baking tray, drizzle over half the oil, sprinkle with a couple of pinches each salt and pepper and mix to evenly coat the tomato halves with oil and seasoning, then bake until softened and slightly wilted, about 25 minutes.

While the tomatoes are roasting, heat the remaining oil in heavy-bottomed pot over medium heat. Add the onion and cook until softened, about 5 minutes. Stir in the crumbled sausage, garlic and chilli. Cook, stirring, until the onion is pale yellow, 5 to 10 minutes. Stir in the beans and stock, bring to the boil, adjust the heat to a steady simmer and cook for 10 minutes.

Take the tomatoes from the oven and drizzle with the balsamic vinegar. Tip the tomatoes and all their juices into the pot and stir in half the parsley or basil. Ladle out a cupful of the beans and tomatoes without too much liquid, put into a food processor, pulse until smooth and stir back in to give the soup a creamier consistency. Or, whiz the soup briefly with one of those hand-held blenders to give it a little body. Return to the heat and simmer steadily for 10 minutes to allow the flavours to blend.

Thin with stock or water as needed. Stir in the rest of the herbs and adjust the seasoning, adding salt, pepper, chilli and balsamic vinegar to taste. Ladle into warmed bowls, drizzle with a little oil and serve hot.

INGREDIENTS NOTE

If you want to use dried beans, you will need 125 g (4 oz/¹/₂ cup). Put in a bowl, cover with water and soak overnight. Drain, rinse and put the soaked beans in a large pan with fresh water to cover by at least 2 cm (1 inch). Bring to the boil and boil hard for 5 minutes. Put on the lid, adjust the heat to a steady simmer and cook the beans are tender, 1 to 1¹/₂ hours. You can use the bean cooking liquor in place of the stock.

HAM HOCK & SPLIT PEA SOUP

Truly a soup to come home to on a cold winter's eve, we were delighted to find this old family favourite in Tom Norrington Davies' irresistible homage to comfort cooking *Just Like Mother Used To Make.*

Bear in mind that not all butchers carry ham hocks all of the time so you might want to order one a couple of days ahead. The time-thrifty among you might like to buy two hocks and up the quantity of celery sticks and carrots (say, eight of each), meaning you squeeze out two different courses or separate meals from one cooking session by making the soup with only the peas and ham broth and serving the ham and vegetables separately - with hot English mustard, of course!

In *Avoca Café Cookbook 2* by Hugo Arnold and Leylie Hayes, a similar ham and pea soup is served topped with a jazzy mint and mustard relish, which you might like to try. Combine 1 tbsp lemon juice, $^1/_2$ tsp black mustard seeds, 1 tbsp finely chopped fresh mint, 1 tbsp finely chopped red onion, 1 finely diced ripe tomato and 1 tbsp olive oil.

SERVES 8

1 organic ham hock
2 onions, halved
4 celery sticks
2 carrots
500 g (1 1lb/2 $^1/_3$ cups) split peas
salt, black pepper

PUT THE HAM, onion, celery, carrots and split peas with 1 $^1/_2$ litres (2 $^1/_2$ pints/6 cups) of water in a large pan over a low heat. Bring slowly to the boil, skimming off any scum that rises to the surface. Adjust the heat and simmer gently until the peas are tender, 2 to 3 hours, topping up with water as needed. Scoop out the ham hock, pull the meat off the bone, discarding the bone and any fatty bits. Put the peas, vegetables and broth in a food processor (you may have to do this in batches) and pulse until smooth-ish. Return to the rinsed out pot with the ham bits and thin with hot water or stock as needed. Reheat gently and add salt and pepper to taste.

ROAST PUMPKIN, GARLIC & ROSEMARY SOUP WITH FETA

A most delicious and beautiful soup – orange squash, white feta, green parsley – from the excellent *A World in My Kitchen* by Peter Gordon. It doesn't have to be parsley, any chopped fresh green herb will do - coriander (cilantro), mint, dill, it's up to you.

SERVES 4

1 kg (2 lb) pumpkin or butternut squash, cut into chunks
12 garlic cloves, halved
2 onions, sliced
1 tbsp roughly chopped fresh rosemary
6 tbsp olive oil
salt, crushed chilli flakes
750 ml (1 pint 4 fl oz/3 cups) hot chicken or vegetable stock
2 tbsp pumpkin seeds
100 g (3 ¹/₂ oz) feta, crumbled
1 tbsp chopped fresh flat-leaf parsley

HEAT THE OVEN to 180 C (350 F) Gas 4. Put the pumpkin, garlic, onion, rosemary and oil in a baking tray and sprinkle with a couple of pinches each salt and chilli. Mix well so that the pumpkin is evenly coated with the oil and roast until the pumpkin, onions and garlic are tender and lightly caramelized, about 45 minutes. Tip the pumpkin into large pan, add a cupful of stock and, using a hand-held blender, whiz to a rough purée. If you don't have a hand-held blender, use a potato masher or transfer to a food processor and use the pulse button. Rinse out the baking dish with the remaining stock so as to dissolve and include any nice oily caramelized bits, add to the pan and bring to a slow simmer over medium heat. Correct the seasoning and adjust the consistency with hot water as needed. Simmer gently to allow the flavours to blend, about 10 minutes.

Toast the pumpkin seeds in a dry frying pan over medium heat until nutty, about 5 minutes. Ladle the soup into warmed bowls, sprinkle with feta, pumpkin seeds and parsley and serve at once.

FARRO & BORLOTTI SOUP

We are increasingly asked for recipes that use farro or spelt - in fact one Saturday, three customers came in consecutively, so we were most pleased to see this robust and heart-warming soup included in Ursula's wonderful *Bringing Italy Home.*

Farro, as Ursula explains, is an ancient grain (cultivated by the Assyrians, Egyptians and Romans, no less) that is planted on graduated terraces in the mountainous Garfagnana region of Tuscany. There are two types available: farro and farricello, which we usually call spelt. It takes about 1 ¹/₂ to 2 hours to cook until tender. Alternatively, you can soak it overnight and it will be ready in about half the time. Look out for farro and spelt in delis, health food shops and Italian stores, but if you can't track either down, buy pearl barley and see the recipe below for Barley and Borlotti Soup.

The pancetta is Eric's addition (like a true Frenchman, he tries to squeeze meaty bits into everything), but can be left out.

SERVES 4

FOR THE BEANS
125 g (4 oz/²/₃ cups) dried borlotti beans, soaked overnight
1 onion
2 garlic cloves
2 fresh sage leaves

FOR THE SOUP
3 tbsp olive oil
125 g (4 oz) pancetta or organic streaky bacon, preferably in a piece, rind removed, diced
1 red onion, finely chopped
2 garlic cloves, finely chopped
1 carrot, chopped
2 celery stalks, chopped
2 fresh sage leaves, finely chopped
1 handful fresh flat-leaf parsley, chopped
90 g (3 oz/¹/₂ cup) farro or spelt, soaked overnight, drained and rinsed,
salt, black pepper
more olive oil to serve

DRAIN THE BEANS, then rinse and put in a large pan with fresh water to cover by at least 2 cm (1 inch). Bring to the boil and boil hard for 5 minutes. Add the onion, garlic and sage, put on the lid, adjust the heat to a steady simmer and cook until the beans are tender, 1 to 1 1/2 hours. When the beans are cooked, scoop out about half the beans and set aside. Place the rest of the beans with their liquor and the onion, garlic and sage in a food processor (you may have to do this in batches) and pulse until smooth.

Warm the oil in the rinsed out pan over medium heat. Add the pancetta or bacon (if using), onion, garlic, carrot, celery, sage and half the parsley and cook until the onion is soft and pale gold, 5 to 10 minutes. Add the soaked grains and the whizzed and whole beans. Thin with hot stock or water as needed. Adjust the heat and simmer gently until the grains are tender, about 45 minutes. Season to taste with salt and pepper and stir in the rest of the parsley. Ladle into warmed bowls, trickle over a little oil and serve at once.

BARLEY & BORLOTTI SOUP

Use 90 g (3 oz/ 1/2 cup) pearl barley instead of the farro or spelt; there's no need to soak the barley, just add it to the vegetables with the whizzed and whole beans and cook as directed.

TOMATO & TAMARIND SOUP WITH TOASTED SPICES

This is an immensely restorative soup - its brightly spiced zingy-ness would perk anyone up. Indeed it is the "chicken soup" of India, where it is known as rasam. Recipes abound but this version of Jennifer's, from her *Small Bites*, gets our vote.

SERVES 4

FOR THE SOUP
2 – 400 g (14 oz) tins chopped Italian plum tomatoes
8 garlic cloves
5 cm (2 inch) piece fresh ginger, sliced
1 tbsp tamarind concentrate (see ingredients note below)
1 1/2 tbsp soft brown sugar
1 tsp turmeric powder
1 tsp salt
1/2 tsp ground black pepper
crushed chilli flakes
900 ml (1 1/2 pints/3 3/4 cups) chicken or vegetable stock
1 handful fresh coriander (cilantro) finely chopped
2 tbsp fresh coriander leaves
4 tbsp thick, creamy yoghurt to serve

FOR THE SPICES
4 tbsp sunflower or olive oil
2 tsp mustard seeds
1 tsp cumin seeds
1 tsp fennel seeds
1/4 tsp crushed chilli flakes
asafoetida (optional – see ingredients note below)

PUT THE TOMATOES, garlic, and ginger in a food processor and pulse until smooth. Pour into a large pan and stir in the tamarind, sugar, turmeric, salt, pepper and a pinch of chilli. Use the stock to rinse out the food processor and pour into the pan. Bring the soup to the boil over medium heat and simmer steadily for 10 minutes. Add the chopped coriander and simmer for another 5 minutes. Taste and add salt and pepper as needed – bearing in mind that you're going to be injecting the soup with a boost of spicy heat with the toasted spiced oil.

Warm the oil in a frying pan over medium heat, add the mustard seeds and cook until they start to crackle and pop, about 2 minutes. Add the chilli, cumin and fennel seeds and a pinch of asafoetida, if using, and fry until spicily fragrant, about 1 minute. Ladle the soup into warmed bowls, drop in a spoonful of yoghurt, spoon in a swirl of the spicy seeded oil and scatter with coriander leaves. Serve at once with warm flatbread.

INGREDIENTS NOTE
Tamarind concentrate is available in pots and keeps indefinitely in the fridge. You can buy it from our neighbour The Spice Shop or at Asian or Middle Eastern food shops.

You can certainly use tamarind pulp instead of tamarind concentrate. Reduce the stock down to 600 ml (1 pint/2 ½ cups). Place 150 g (5 oz) dried tamarind pulp in a small bowl, cover with 300 m. (10 fl oz/1 ¼ cups) boiling water and leave to soak until cool enough to handle, about 15 minutes. Squeeze hard to dissolve the pulp in the water, rubbing between your fingers dissolve as much as possible, then strain and discard the seeds and fibres.

Asafoetida is the dried and ground root of the giant fennel plant. In India it's as much used for its medicinal, digestive properties as its distinctive flavour.

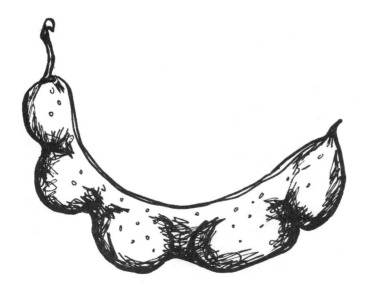

COURGETTE, GOAT CHEESE & BASIL SOUP

A truly heavenly summer soup from Hugh Fearnley-Whittingstall and his *The River Cottage Year.*

SERVES 4

3 tbsp olive oil
2 garlic cloves, finely chopped
1 kg (2 lb) courgettes (zucchini), sliced $^1/_2$ cm ($^1/_4$ inch) thick
100 g (3 $^1/_2$ oz) fresh goat's cheese
600 ml (1 pint/ 2 $^1/_2$ cups) hot milk
salt, black pepper
1 handful fresh basil, leaves torn if necessary

WARM THE OIL in a large pan over medium heat. Add the garlic and cook until fragrant and pale gold, 3 minutes. Stir in the courgettes, reduce the heat to low and stew slowly, stirring fairly frequently, until meltingly tender, but not coloured, about 20 minutes. Remove from the heat, add the goat's cheese and, using a hand-held blender, whiz to a rough purée. If you don't have a hand-held blender, use a potato masher or transfer to a food processor and use the pulse button. Stir the milk into the soup and bring to a slow simmer over medium heat. Add salt and pepper to taste and adjust the consistency with more milk or water as needed. Serve hot, warm or chilled, as temperature and occasion requires, scattered with the basil.

LENTIL & CHORIZO SOUP

This robustly flavoured soup often features on the Saturday menus at Books for Cooks as it's a real crowd-pleaser. It's possibly our favourite lentil soup of all time (thank you Eric!).

SERVES 4

30 g (1 oz/2 tbsp) butter
1 onion, chopped
2 carrots, chopped
3 garlic cloves, chopped
2 celery sticks, chopped
100 g (3 1/2 oz) chorizo, skinned and chopped
175 g (6 oz/1 cup) puy lentils
1 litre (1 3/4 pints/4 cups) hot chicken or vegetable stock
150 ml (5 fl oz/2/3 cup) crème fraîche
salt, black pepper
1 tbsp finely chopped fresh flat-leaf parsley

MELT THE BUTTER in a large pan over medium heat, add the onion, carrot, garlic, celery and chorizo and cook, stirring once or twice, until the onion is soft and pale gold, 5 to 10 minutes. Stir in the lentils, pour over the stock, bring to the boil, adjust the heat and simmer steadily for 50 minutes. Place in a food processor (you may have to do this in batches) and pulse until silky smooth. Return to the rinsed out pan, stir in the cream and thin with hot water or stock as needed. Add salt and pepper to taste, ladle into warmed bowls, sprinkle with parsley and serve hot.

FENNEL SOUP WITH ORANGE GREMOLATA

Food-writing duo Canadian Lindsay Wilson and New Zealander Pippa Cuthbert met right here in London over the stoves and among the bookshelves at Books for Cooks. They have so far collaborated on three colourful cookbooks bursting with fast and fabulous flavours – *Juice!, Ice Cream* and their latest *Soup* from where this recipe comes.

They write… "Gremolata is an Italian garnish of parsley, garlic and lemon zest traditionally sprinkled over osso bucco. Here we take it to another level, substituting orange zest for lemon and pairing it with a velvety fennel soup – a fresh, inspired combination."

SERVES 4

15 g (¹/₂ oz/1 tbsp) butter
1 tbsp olive oil
2 onions, chopped
1 clove garlic, chopped
2 leeks, whites and pale green parts only, chopped
1 fennel bulb, chopped (reserve the green fronds to make the
    gremolata garnish)
small glass white wine
900 ml (1 ¹/₂ pints/3 ³/₄ cups) hot chicken or vegetable stock
salt, black pepper, freshly grated nutmeg
250 ml (8 fl oz/1 cup) single (light) cream
2 tsp aniseed-flavoured aperitif such as Ricard or Pernod

FOR THE GREMOLATA
2 tbsp finely chopped fresh flat-leaf parsley
finely chopped fennel fronds
2 garlic cloves, finely chopped
grated zest 1 organic orange (wash and scrub well if not organic)
1 tbsp olive oil

MELT THE BUTTER with the oil in a large pan, add the onion, garlic, leeks and fennel and cook, stirring once or twice, until softened but not coloured, 10 to 15 minutes. Pour in the wine, bring to the boil and bubble furiously for a minute or two to allow the alcohol to evaporate. Pour in the stock, bring to the boil, adjust the heat and simmer steadily until the vegetables are soft, 10-15 minutes. Place in a food processor (you may have to do this in batches) and

20

pulse until silky smooth. Return to the rinsed out pan, stir in the cream and liqueur and thin with hot water or stock as needed. Season to taste with salt, pepper and nutmeg and reheat gently until piping hot.

Make the gremolata. Mix the parsley, fennel fronds, garlic, orange zest and olive oil until evenly combined and add salt and pepper to taste. Ladle the soup into warmed bowls and sprinkle each serving with a spoonful of the orange gremolata. Serve at once.

ALL-SEASON PAPPA AL POMMODORO

A way of using yesterday's bread and sun-ripened tomatoes from the garden, *pappa al pommodoro* is typically thrifty Tuscan peasant fare. Years ago it was near impossible to reproduce here, as it was so difficult to find a decent proper country loaf. Nowadays there's always ciabatta if an independent baker baking slow-risen and naturally leavened bread eludes you, but the tomatoes still pose a problem as most supermarket tomato varieties just aren't good enough to compete with those sweet, ripe, misshapen wonders on market stalls across Europe. But help is now at hand with this clever recipe from Rose Gray and Ruth Rogers' *River Café Cook Book* Easy. The secret of its success is to bypass the tomato problem altogether by using tinned and then slow simmering them until sweetly jammy. You can serve this sturdy soup hot, warm or cold, according to season.

SERVES 4

6 tbsp olive oil
2 garlic cloves, finely sliced
1 tbsp finely chopped fresh sage
250 ml (8 fl oz/1 cup) hot chicken or vegetable stock
250 g (8 oz) day-old ciabatta, pain de campagne or other sourdough bread,
    sliced 1 cm (1/2 inch) thick
2 - 400 g (14 oz) tins chopped Italian plum tomatoes
salt, crushed chilli flakes
2 tbsp freshly grated Parmesan (the pre-grated stuff will not do)
more olive oil to serve

WARM THE OIL in a large pan over high heat. Add the garlic and sage and cook until the garlic starts to colour, about 3 minutes. Add the stock and the bread and stir to roughly break up the bread – don't overwork, you're aiming for a chunky texture, not complete mush. Cook until the bread soaks up the stock and starts to sizzle and crisp, about 5 minutes.

Add the tomatoes and stir to combine the bread and the tomatoes. Lower the heat and let simmer steadily until the tomatoes cook down until thick and jammy, about 15 minutes. Stir in enough hot stock or water (you'll only need a cupful or two) to loosen the soup – you're aiming for a thick and sturdy rather than a liquid consistency. Season to taste with salt and chilli. Spoon into warmed bowls and serve at once with a sprinkling of Parmesan and a swirl of olive oil.

ROAST SWEET POTATO SOUP
WITH SPICY THAI FLAVOURS

You can certainly use this spicy, creamy, tangy coconut soup from *Avoca Café Cookbook 2* by Hugo Arnold and Leylie Hayes as a blueprint broth for vegetables other than sweet potatoes. To continue in the orange theme, try roast pumpkin or carrot, see red with a duo of roast peppers and cherry tomatoes, or go green with a trio of broccoli florets, frozen peas and baby spinach. Simply add soaked rice noodles for a more substantial repast.

SERVES 4

500 g (1 lb) sweet potatoes, cut into 2 ¹/₂ cm (1 inch) cubes
4 tbsp sunflower oil
1 onion, finely sliced
2 leeks, white and tender green part only, finely sliced
2 cm (³/₄ inch) piece fresh ginger, finely sliced
1 fresh green chilli, seeded and finely sliced
2 lemon grass stalks, tender inner white part only, finely sliced
4 kaffir lime leaves, finely sliced
1 litre (1 ³/₄ pints/4 cups) chicken or vegetable stock
250 ml (8 fl oz/1 cup) coconut milk (don't forget to shake the tin well
      before opening)
2 tbsp fish sauce
2 tbsp torn fresh basil leaves, preferably Thai

HEAT THE OVEN to 200 C (400 F) Gas 6. Put the sweet potatoes in a baking tray, drizzle with 2 tablespoons of the oil and mix well so that the potatoes are evenly coated with the oil. Roast until tender, about 20 minutes.

Put the remaining oil in a large pan over high heat. When the oil is hot, add the onion and stir-fry until soft and golden, about 4 minutes. Stir in the leeks, ginger, chilli, lemon grass, lime leaves and pour in the stock. Bring to a steady simmer, adjust the heat and let bubble gently until the leeks are tender, about 15 minutes. Ladle out a cupful of the soup, put into a food processor, pulse until smooth and stir back in to give the soup a creamier consistency. Or, whiz the soup briefly with one of those hand held blenders to give it a little body. Tip the sweet potatoes into the soup and stir in the coconut milk and fish sauce. Taste for saltiness, adding more fish sauce as needed. Reheat gently until piping hot, ladle into warmed bowls, scatter with basil and serve at once.

SAFFRON, TAHINI & YOGHURT SOUP

Combining the nutty taste of tahini, the pungent aroma of saffron, the sharpness of yoghurt and the zestiness of lemon, this is a rather special soup from *Casa Moro* by the Sams Clark.

Its velvety texture is achieved with an egg liason, so the finished soup must not boil. If the phone does ring and you do allow the soup to boil and it splits, it can be salvaged, although it won't be so unctuously creamy as before. Blend half a tablespoon of cornflour with two tablespoons of water or stock, whisk into the soup and simmer gently for 5 minutes. Whiz in batches at top speed in a food processor, than pass through your finest sieve back into the saucepan. Thin with hot stock or water as needed, reheat gently and don't let it boil again!

SERVES 4

$^1/_2$ tsp saffron strands
1 garlic clove
1 tsp coarse salt
1 organic egg yolk
$^1/_2$ tbsp cornflour (cornstarch)
500 ml (16 fl oz/2 cups) thick, creamy yoghurt
3 tbsp tahini
2 tbsp olive oil
grated zest and juice $^1/_2$ organic lemon (wash and scrub well if not organic)
750 ml (1 pint 4 fl oz/3 cups) chicken or vegetable stock
3 tbsp chopped fresh flat-leaf parsley
2 tbsp chopped fresh dill
1 tbsp chopped fresh mint
salt, black pepper

PUT THE SAFFRON in a bowl with two tablespoons of boiling water and leave to infuse for 30 minutes. Crush the garlic clove with the salt to a smooth paste – do this in with a pestle and mortar or place the garlic on a chopping board, sprinkle over the salt and work the flat side of a chef's knife over the garlic until completely smooth.

Put the egg yolk in a large mixing bowl, sift over the cornflour and whisk in until smoothly combined. This egg-and-starch mix enriches, thickens and binds the soup so that the yoghurt doesn't curdle when heated. Now whisk in the yoghurt, tahini, oil, salty garlic and lemon until well mixed. Gradually whisk

24

into the stock or water until smoothly combined. Pour into a heavy-bottomed pan and, stirring occasionally, gently and carefully warm the soup over a low heat until piping but not simmering hot – don't let it bubble or it will split!

Off the heat, stir in about half the saffron liquor with the fresh herbs. Taste and adjust the seasoning with salt, pepper and more lemon if necessary. Ladle into warmed bowls, spoon a swirl of the remaining saffron liquor on top and serve at once.

CHICKEN & ROAST PEPPER SOUP WITH BASIL

A satisfying soulful soup from Ursula's *Trattoria*. If you can't find fresh basil, use flat-leaf parsley instead. If you can't find fresh marjoram or oregano, add half a teaspoonful of dried oregano to the pan with the peppers.

SERVES 4

6 red peppers, halved
5 tbsp olive oil
salt
4 organic chicken thighs
1 onion, finely chopped
2 garlic cloves, crushed
$1/4$ tsp crushed chilli flakes
600 ml (1 pint/2 $1/2$ cups) hot chicken or vegetable stock
1 handful fresh basil leaves, sliced
2 tsp fresh marjoram or oregano, chopped
more olive oil to serve

HEAT THE OVEN to 190 C (375 F) Gas 5. Arrange the pepper halves snugly in a crowded single layer in a baking dish. Drizzle over four tablespoons oil and sprinkle with salt. Roast until very soft, about 40 minutes, stirring and basting at least twice to ensure that the peppers emerge succulent and juicy. Remove from the oven and cover with dish with a baking sheet to allow the trapped steam to loosen the pepper skins so they can easily be slipped off. While the peppers are roasting, place the chicken thighs in another baking dish, sprinkle with salt and roast until cooked through with no hint of pink, about 30 minutes.

When cool enough to handle, slip the skins off the peppers and discard, then slice the peppers into strips, reserving any oily juices. Remove the skin and bones from the chicken and discard, then slice the chicken into strips. Warm the remaining tablespoon of oil with a tablespoon of water in a large pan over medium heat, add the onion and cook, stirring once or twice, until soft and pale gold, 5 to 10 minutes. Stir in the garlic, chilli and peppers with their juices and cook until sizzling and fragrant, about 3 minutes. Pour in the hot stock, bring just to the boil, adjust the heat and simmer gently for 5 minutes to allow the flavours to blend. Stir in the fresh herbs and chicken, check the seasoning and adjust the consistency with hot stock or water as needed. Serve hot in warmed bowls with a trickle of your best olive oil.

Main Courses

SMOKED HADDOCK, LEEK & POTATO PIE

We're very partial to pies, as readers of *Books for Cooks 5* and *6* can attest, so were delighted to discover this recipe *Avoca Café Cookbook 2* by Hugo Arnold and Leylie Hayes. A cursory first glance at the ingredients list might have you dismissing this dish as old news, but bear with us, this is a fish pie with a difference. The potatoes are diced and added to the creamy fish filling rather than mashed and used as topping and the whole concoction is baked in a pastry crust until golden and tempting.

SERVES 4-6

2 medium potatoes (about 250 g/8 oz)
350 g (12 oz) smoked haddock
250 ml (8 fl oz/1 cup) milk
$^1/_4$ tsp saffron threads
250 ml (8 fl oz/1 cup double (heavy) cream or crème fraîche
60 g (2 oz/4 tbsp) butter
2 medium leeks, chopped (about 300 g/10 oz)
30 g (1 oz/3 tbsp) flour
Salt, black pepper, grated nutmeg
2 tbsp freshly grated Parmesan, Gruyère or strong Cheddar

24 cm (9 $^1/_2$ inch) shortcrust pastry case, baked blind (pre-baked) (see pages 104-106)

HEAT THE OVEN to 180 C (350 F) Gas 4.

Cut the potatoes into even dice and cook in boiling salted water until tender, about 10 minutes.

Put the haddock and the milk in a wide, shallow pan over low heat and bring slowly to simmering point. Simmer gently for 5 minutes, then take the pan off the heat and let the fish cool slightly in the milk. Flake the cooked fish from the bones and skin and reserve. Add the saffron and cream to the milk and set aside.

Melt the butter in a heavy-bottomed pan over low heat, add the leeks and cook gently until wilted and soft but not coloured, about 10 minutes. Stir in flour and cook for 1 minute. Stir in the saffron-tinted milk and cream and, still stirring, bring to a gentle simmer and keep stirring until the mixture thickens.

Simmer gently for another 5 minutes. Remove from the heat, stir in the haddock and potatoes and season to taste with salt, pepper and nutmeg. Spread evenly in the pastry case, sprinkle with cheese and grind over a little extra pepper. Bake until golden, crusty and tempting, about 20 minutes. Serve hot or warm with a watercress salad dressed with a mustardy vinaigrette (see Jennifer's essential *The Well-Dressed Salad* for her fabulous Grainy Mustard Vinaigrette and indeed the ultimate salad dressing collection!).

RICOTTA GNOCCHI WITH GORGONZOLA SAUCE

Deliciously light and fluffy, these gnocchi are a breeze to make and can even be made ahead of time. We found them in Ursula's *Italy Sea to Sky* and she suggests serving them with a crisp green leaf salad.

SERVES 4

400 g (14 oz) ricotta
3 organic egg yolks
2 tbsp freshly grated Parmesan (the pre-grated stuff will not do)
5 tbsp semolina
$^{1}/_{4}$ tsp each salt and black pepper
freshly grated nutmeg

FOR THE SAUCE
15 g ($^{1}/_{2}$ oz/1 tbsp) butter
2 tbsp double (heavy) cream
100 g (3 $^{1}/_{2}$ oz) Gorgonzola cheese, crumbled
1 tbsp finely chopped fresh flat-leaf parsley

PUT THE RICOTTA with the eggs, Parmesan, semolina, salt, pepper and a couple of good pinches of nutmeg in a large bowl and mix thoroughly to make a dough. On a lightly oiled surface (you could use a plastic tray or large chopping board if you don't want to oil your work surface), roll the dough into thin sausages about as thick as your thumb, then cut the rolls with a sharp knife into lengths about 2 cm ($^{3}/_{4}$ inch) long.

For the sauce, melt the butter with the cream in a saucepan over a low heat. Add the Gorgonzola and mash and stir with a wooden spoon until the butter, cream and cheese are thick and creamy, about 1 minute. Turn off the heat and set aside until you are ready to cook the gnocchi.

Bring a large pan of salted water to the boil and adjust the heat so that the water gently simmers, not boils. Lower the gnocchi, one at a time, on a slotted spoon into the simmering water and poach until they float back to the surface, about 2 minutes. Remove with a slotted spoon to a warmed serving dish. Drop more dumplings into the pan and repeat the whole operation.

Briefly warm through the sauce, pour over the gnocchi, sprinkle with parsley

Briefly warm through the sauce, pour over the gnocchi, sprinkle with parsley and serve at once.

RICOTTA GNOCCHI WITH PINE NUTS & FRESH BASIL
An alternative garnish for these feather-light dumplings. Toast 50 g (scant 2 oz/6 tbsp) pine nuts in a dry pan over low heat until nutty and golden, about 5 minutes. When the gnocchi are all cooked, quickly melt 30 g (1 oz) butter and, when it is sizzling hot, pour over the gnocchi. Scatter over the toasted pine nuts, a handful of fresh torn basil leaves and 2 tbsp freshly grated Parmesan and serve at once.

THINK AHEAD
These gnocchi can be made a day ahead, as long as they are kept covered and in single layers, not touching, in the refrigerator.

MAGHREBI MEATBALLS WITH SPINACH & CHICKPEAS

We at Books for Cooks have been conducting a passionate culinary love affair with Paula Wolfert's *The Slow Mediterranean Kitchen* for some time. When the team sat down in June to discuss which books and their recipes were to feature in this little book, narrowing our recipe selection down to just one proved quite a challenge and the subject of some heated discussion. Finally, we plumped for this succulent and subtly spiced meatball stew as being the most Books for Cooks-y kind of dish.

SERVES 4

FOR THE MEATBALLS
1 ^{1}/$_2$ slices bread, crusts cut off, cubed
6 garlic cloves, crushed
4 tsp ground coriander
4 tsp sweet paprika
1 tsp salt
^{1}/$_2$ tsp freshly ground black pepper
^{1}/$_8$ tsp ground cumin
^{1}/$_8$ tsp ground turmeric
^{1}/$_8$ tsp cayenne
^{1}/$_8$ tsp ground caraway
375 g (12 oz) organic minced lamb, pork or beef or a mixture of pork and beef
2 tbsp chopped flat-leaf parsley
1 organic egg yolk

FOR THE STEW
3 tbsp olive oil
2 onions, chopped
200 g (7 oz) tin chopped Italian plum tomatoes
400 g (14 oz) tin chickpeas, drained
^{1}/$_4$ tsp saffron threads
250 ml (8 fl oz/1 cup) hot chicken or vegetable stock or water
500 g (1 lb) spinach
1 handful chopped flat-leaf parsley
salt, black pepper

MAKE THE MEATBALLS. Soak the bread in 4 tbsp of water for 10 minutes, then squeeze dry. Place the garlic, coriander, paprika, salt, pepper, cumin, turmeric, cayenne, and caraway in a food processor with 2 tbsp of water and whiz to a paste. Add the minced meat, squeezed bread, parsley and egg yolk and pulse until well combined. With wet hands (to stop the mixture sticking), divide the mixture into 32 equal-sized pieces and roll into walnut-sized balls. Arrange on a baking tray and chill for 20 minutes.

Warm the oil over medium-high heat in a wide, heavy-bottomed pot until it sizzles. Add the meatballs and fry a few at a time for about 5 minutes, turning them so that they are crisp and browned all over. Remove from the pot and set aside.

Add the onions to the pot with 2 tbsp of water and cook until the water has bubbled away and the onions are soft and lightly golden, about 5 minutes. Stir in the tomatoes and let bubble down until the juices have concentrated, about 5 minutes. Add the chickpeas, meatballs and saffron to the pot and pour in the hot stock or water. Bring to the boil, adjust the heat, put on the lid and simmer gently for 30 minutes.

If you're using proper spinach from the garden or the market, wash the spinach first, then pile the still wet leaves into a large pan, put on the lid and cook over a medium heat until the spinach starts to wilt, about 2 minutes. You don't need any water in the pan, as the water still clinging to the spinach leaves will create enough steam to cook the spinach. Stir the spinach, put the lid back on and continue cooking until tender, 1-2 minutes. Drain and, when cool enough to handle. Squeeze lightly to remove any wateriness and chop roughly.

If you're using supermarket or baby spinach, it's so tender and cooks so speedily that you can add the spinach directly to the stew.

When the stew has simmered for half an hour, gently fold in the spinach and parsley and cook, uncovered, for 10 minutes to allow the flavours to blend. Add salt and pepper to taste and serve hot, in warmed bowls, with buttered couscous, Garlic Rice (see page 73) or plenty of warm flatbread.

PASTA WITH PORCINI CHICKEN SAUCE

Ursula created a tamer version of the famous Tuscan dish *pappardelle con leper* (thick ribbon pasta with hare sauce) by using rabbit instead of hare. You'll find the original recipe in her truly essential *Truly Madly Pasta,* but we then tamed her version of this Italian classic still further by using chicken instead. Don't be tempted to substitute breast for the tastier brown meat and do choose proper chicken (buy organic or from a trusted producer at a farmers' market or the farm gate) to achieve the full flavour of this most delicious dish.

SERVES 4

30 g (1 oz/1 cup) dried porcini mushrooms
30 g (1 oz/2 tbsp) butter
1 tbsp olive oil
1 onion, finely chopped
1 carrot, finely chopped
1 celery stalk, finely chopped
60 g (2 oz) pancetta, diced, or 2 organic streaky bacon rashers, chopped
1 handful fresh flat-leaf parsley, roughly chopped
250 g (8 oz) boned and skinned brown organic chicken meat (leg, thigh or drumstick)
small glass white wine
400 g (14 oz) tin chopped Italian plum tomatoes
3 fresh or 2 dry bay leaves
salt, black pepper
400 g (14 oz) pasta

Soak the dried porcini in 175 ml (6 fl oz/³/₄ cup) hand-hot water for about half an hour. Scoop out, squeezing out as much water as possible and chop finely. Strain the soaking liquid through kitchen paper and set aside.

Melt the butter with the oil in a heavy pot (with a lid) over medium heat. Add the onion, carrot, celery, pancetta or bacon and most of the parsley (keep some for sprinkling) and cook, stirring until soft and lightly coloured, about 5 minutes.

Add the chicken and fry until lightly browned on both sides, about 4 minutes. Pour over the wine, let bubble until slightly reduced, about 2 minutes. Stir in the tomatoes, bay leaves, porcini and pour in the soaking liquid. Stir well to mix everything together, then cover, adjust the heat and simmer slowly, stirring from time to time, until the chicken is really tender, about 45 minutes.

Remove the pot from the heat and scoop out the chicken. Cut into bite-size chunks and stir back into the sauce. Fish out the bay leaves and season the sauce to taste. Simmer gently for 10 minutes to allow the flavours to blend.

Cook the pasta in plenty of boiling salted water (use the instructions on the packet as a guide but start testing a couple of minutes before the suggested time is up) until *al dente,* that is, just tender but still firm to the bite. Drain the pasta and add to the sauce with the rest of the parsley. Toss well to coat and serve straightaway.

THINK AHEAD
You can certainly make the sauce a day ahead – in fact it definitely improves in flavour for it. Let cool completely, then cover and chill. Reheat, then add the cooked pasta.

AROMATIC PORK BELLY HOT POT

To be blunt, we maintain that no keen cook or good food lover (excepting the veggies amongst you of course) can afford to be without our favourite food hero Hugh Fearnley Whittingstall's monumental *The River Cottage Meat Book*. Indeed, if the thought-provoking opening section "Understanding Meat" was mandatory reading for all butchers, farmers, supermarket meat buyers and anyone remotely connected with the meat industry, the world just might be a better place. But this five-hundred-odd page tome is more than food for thought, it's quite simply chock-a-block with just about everything you'd ever need to know about cooking meat, poultry and game – plus all the offal-y bits - with recipes that range all the way from hog roasts to leftovers. Among our many meaty favourites is this slow simmered, meltingly tender pork dish.

SERVES 4-6

1 ½ kg (3 lb) boned organic belly pork, with skin on
1 litre (1 ¾ pints/4 cups) hot chicken stock
6 spring onions
90 ml (3 fl oz/⅓ cup + 1 tbsp) soy sauce
5 tbsp Chinese rice wine
2 tbsp rice wine vinegar
2 tbsp light brown sugar
3 star anise
10 cm (4 inch) piece fresh ginger, finely sliced
¼ tsp dried chilli flakes
4 extra spring onions, finely sliced on the diagonal, to garnish

CUT THE PORK into 2 ½ by 5 cm (1 by 2 inch) pieces (you're using proper, free-ranging, organic pork, you may need a sharp serrated knife or sturdy kitchen scissors to cut through the skin). Place in a large pot (with a lid) and pour over just enough boiling water to cover. Bring to the boil over medium-low heat and simmer gently for 5 minutes, skimming off any scum. Drain, discarding the water, and return the pork to the rinsed out pan. Pour over the stock and add the spring onions, soy, rice wine and vinegar, sugar, star anise, ginger and chilli. Bring back to the boil, put on the lid and adjust the heat to a slow simmer. Cook very gently, with the stock barely bubbling, stirring from time to time, until the pork is meltingly tender, about 2 hours. Alternatively, put into a preheated 150 C (300 F) Gas 2 oven to stew slowly.

Scoop out the pork and set aside. Strain the stock through a sieve and skim off as much fat as you can. Return the stock to the rinsed out pan, bring to the boil over medium heat and let bubble fiercely to reduce the stock by about a quarter. Tip the pork back into the aromatic stock, adjust the seasoning with more soy and chilli as needed and heat through. Ladle into warmed bowls over Asian noodles (cook according to the instructions on the packet) or steamed rice, sprinkle with spring onions and serve at once.

AUBERGINES WITH SPICED WALNUT SAUCE

This punchy and nutritious sauce comes from Celia's magnum opus *World Vegetarian Classics* and hails originally from Georgia. There, as Celia says, it is served with all manner of fish, fowl and vegetables but has a special partnership with fried aubergines. Celia suggests serving with rice or bulgur (see page 72 for Sam and Sam Clark's Red Pepper Bulgur) and a leafy salad for a well-rounded vegetarian meal. Scattering the dish with ruby pomegranate seeds is traditional and most decorative, but if pomegranates are out of season, don't let that put you off making this delicious dish.

SERVES 4

500 g (1 lb) aubergines (eggplants) (3 smallish or 2 medium),
salt, black pepper
sunflower oil for frying
100 g (3 ¹/₂ oz/1 cup) walnuts
1 tbsp red wine vinegar
1 clove garlic, quartered
1 tsp hot paprika
1 tsp ground coriander
3 tbsp roughly chopped fresh coriander (cilantro)
125-150 ml (4-5 fl oz/ ¹/₄ -¹/₃ cup) tepid water
fresh pomegranate seeds to garnish, when available

Slice the aubergines into lengths no more than ³/₄ cm (¹/₃ inch) thick. Sprinkle lightly with salt and leave in a colander for 20 minutes to drain, then blot the aubergines dry well on kitchen paper.

Heat a shallow pool of sunflower oil in a large frying pan over medium heat. It is ready for frying when a piece of bread added to the pan sizzles immediately. While it is heating, pat the aubergines dry once more just before slipping them into the hot oil. Add only as many slices as needed to make a single layer. Fry, turning with tongs, until soft and light golden but not crisp or brittle on both sides. Remove with a slotted spatula, drain off any excess oil on kitchen paper, then sprinkle with salt and leave to cool while you fry the remaining aubergine slices.

Make the sauce. Put the walnuts, vinegar, garlic, paprika, ground and most of the fresh coriander (save a sprinkling to garnish the dish) in a food processor or blender. With the motor running, pour in water gradually, adding just enough to make a thick, smooth, barely pourable paste. Season to taste.

Take each aubergine slice and place a heaped teaspoonful of the walnut sauce at one end. Fold the aubergine over the sauce, and top with another spoonful. If the aubergine slices are long enough, fold back over the paste again, making an S-shape, and top again with the sauce.

Arrange on a platter. Sprinkle with coarsely chopped coriander and pomegranate seeds. Serve as soon as possible, as the walnut sauce splits after a while.

SPICY BRAISED OXTAIL

We love Annabel Langbein's cookbooks and we maintain New Zealand's top cookbook author is not nearly as well known outside her native land as she deserves to be. Her most recent cookbook, *Cooking To Impress Without Stress*, is vintage Langbein and is the "prepare-ahead" cookbook we – and so many of our customers – have been clamouring for.

We chose this really tasty, easy dish from *Cooking To Impress Without Stress* to exemplify her special style of fusion food with its typically antipodean twist. A great recipe when cooking for a crowd, it's really the Rolls Royce of chillis, rich and sticky with a voluptuously velvety sauce, and never fails to win applause.

SERVES 8

500 g (1 lb/2 $^1/_2$ cups) pinto, borlotti or red kidney beans soaked overnight
2 kg (5 lb) organic oxtails, cut into short lengths and soaked
      in cold water for 4 hours
salt, black pepper
2 tbsp sunflower or olive oil
2 onions, finely chopped
8 garlic cloves, crushed
5 cm (2 inch) piece fresh ginger, grated
3 – 400 g (14 oz) tins chopped Italian plum tomatoes
175 ml (6 fl oz/$^3/_4$ cup) tomato ketchup
75 g (2 $^1/_2$ oz/$^1/_3$ cup) dark brown sugar
3 tbsp creamy Dijon mustard
150 ml (5 fl oz/$^2/_3$ cup) cider vinegar
1 tbsp Worcestershire sauce
$^1/_2$ tsp cayenne
1 handful fresh flat-leaf parsley, finely chopped, to garnish
Soft Polenta to serve (see page 68)

HEAT THE OVEN to 220 C (425F) Gas 7.

Drain and rinse the soaked beans, then put in a large pan (with a lid), cover with fresh water by at least 2 cm (1 inch) and bring to the boil. Boil hard for 10 minutes, then put on the lid, adjust the heat and simmer steadily for 30 minutes. Take from the heat and drain, reserving 500 ml (16 fl oz/2 cups) bean liquor. Set the beans and the reserved cooking liquid aside while you roast the oxtail.

Drain the oxtail and pat dry with kitchen paper – if you've forgotten to soak the oxtail, just rinse the pieces under cold running water. Arrange the oxtail pieces in a roasting tin in a single layer and season with salt and pepper. Roast until nicely browned, turning once halfway through cooking, about 45 minutes. Take out of the oven, pour off the fat and set the oxtail aside. Turn the oven down to 150 C (300 F) Gas 2.

While the oxtails roast, heat the oil in a wide, heavy-bottomed pot (with a lid) over medium heat. Add the onions and cooking, stirring, until softened and lightly golden, about 10 minutes. Stir in the garlic and ginger and cook until fragrant, about another minute. Add the tomatoes, bring to the boil and, stirring once or twice, let cook down slightly concentrated, about 5 minutes. Stir in the tomato ketchup, sugar, mustard, vinegar, Worcestershire sauce and cayenne. Add the beans and the reserved cooking liquid, bring to the boil, adjust the heat to a steady simmer and cook for 5 minutes.

Add the oxtail to the pot, put on the lid and bake in the oven until the meat is meltingly tender and coming away from the bone, about 3 hours. At this point, Annabel recommends leaving the stew to cool and chilling it overnight, as any fat will have hardened and can easily being lifted off the next day. Let the stew return to room temperature, then reheat in a 150 C (300 F) Gas 2 oven until piping hot, about 1 hour. Check the seasoning, adding salt, pepper and cayenne to taste, and serve hot sprinkled with parsley. If, however, that's one cook-ahead step too far and you want to sup here and now, simply skim off and discard any fat that sits on the surface of the stew with a large spoon before serving.

To serve, Annabel suggests Soft Polenta (turn to page 68 and double the recipe if you're serving eight people). We approve, polenta being a sort of contemporary update on the classic chilli accompaniment, cornbread. However, if you prefer, a creamy root vegetable mash (turn to page 80 in *Favourite Recipes from Books for Cooks 1, 2 & 3)* or Garlic Rice (see page 73 of this little book) would also be just the ticket. A helping of steamed seasonal greens, curly kale, Savoy cabbage or spring greens would complete this substantial repast – or you could simply follow this sticky oxtail stew with a crisp green leaf salad.

INGREDIENTS NOTE
Forgotten to soak the beans? There's no need to reach for tinned! Alongside this recipe Annabel shares this great culinary shortcut – how to fast-soak dried beans. In a large pan (with a lid), cover the beans with four times their volume

water, bring to the boil over medium heat and boil hard for 10 minutes. Remove from the heat and let stand for 40 minutes. Drain well, then return the beans to the pan, cover with fresh water by at least 2 cm (1 inch) and boil hard for 5 minutes. Put on the lid, adjust the heat to a slow simmer and cook until tender, anything from 1 to 1 ½ hours, depending on the age of your beans and the hardness of your water.

THINK AHEAD
This dish is positively benefits from being cooked a day or two or three ahead, as the flavours develop and deepen, plus you also have a chance to lift off the fat when the stew is cold.

CORIANDER CHILLI FISH CURRY

Jennifer put us on to this simple spicy fish stew from Manju Malhi's *India with Passion*. Manju has recently started teaching here at Books for Cooks and we urge you to look out for her workshops on regional Indian cookery.

SERVES 4

1 kg (2 lb) haddock or other white fish fillets, skinned
$^1/_2$ tsp turmeric
2 tsp ground cumin
2 tsp ground coriander
$^1/_2$ tsp salt
2 fresh green chillies, sliced
1 handful fresh coriander (cilantro) leaves, chopped
3 tbsp sunflower oil
$^1/_2$ tsp cumin seeds
1 tsp brown or black mustard seeds
4 garlic cloves, crushed
2 cm ($^3/_4$ inch) piece fresh ginger, grated
1 onion, finely chopped
2 ripe tomatoes, roughly chopped

CUT THE FISH into pieces about 8 cm (3 inches) long. Put the turmeric, ground cumin, ground coriander, salt, chillies and about half the coriander leaves in a bowl and mix to evenly combine. Add the fish pieces and gently mix until the fish is well coated with the spice mixture.

Warm two tablespoons of the oil in a large frying pan over medium high heat. Add the fish and its spice mix and fry until lightly browned on both sides, about 5 minutes. Scoop out and set aside.

Heat the remaining oil in the same pan. Add the cumin and mustard seeds and cook until they pop, about 2 minutes. Turn down the heat to medium, stir in the garlic, ginger, onion and tomatoes and cook until the onion is soft, 5 to 10 minutes. Pour in 300 ml (10 fl oz/1 $^1/_4$ cups) boiling water and let bubble for a minute. Adjust the heat to a gentle simmer and return the fish to the pan. Cook very gently, stirring once or twice for 10 minutes, when the fish will be cooked through and the sauce slightly reduced. Serve at once with steamed basmati rice.

POACHED CHICKEN WITH SWEET SOY, CHILLI & GINGER DIPPING SAUCE

Poaching is a really delicious way of doing justice to a proper free-range organic chicken. We owe this Asian spin on poached poultry to Jennifer who likes to marry the tender, juicy chicken with sweetly sticky soy, garlicky rice cooked in the broth and the cool crunch of cucumber.

SERVES 4

1 organic chicken
1 handful fresh coriander (cilantro), chopped
2 Lebanese cucumbers (see ingredients note below) or 1 medium cucumber, de-seeded
Garlic Rice to serve (see page 73)

FOR THE SAUCE
4 tablespoons ketchap manis (see ingredients note below)
1 fresh red chilli, seeded and finely chopped
2 garlic cloves, crushed
2 ¹/₂ cm (1 inch) piece fresh ginger, grated
1 tbsp rice vinegar
2 tbsp sugar

PUT THE CHICKEN in a large pot (with a lid) and cover completely with water. Bring to the boil and simmer steadily for 10 minutes. Turn off the heat, put on the lid and leave completely undisturbed for 1 hour.

With a vegetable peeler, shave the cucumbers into fine ribbons. Make the dipping sauce by stirring the ketchap manis, chilli, garlic, ginger, vinegar and sugar until well combined.

Take the chicken from the pot, cut into portions and remove all the skin and bones.

Make the Garlic Rice (see page 73) using some of the stock – use the rest to make soup.

You can serve the chicken plated or, more convivially, we think, family-style on a large platter. Divide the chicken among 4 plates or arrange on a single large dish. Garnish with the cucumber ribbons and fresh coriander. Serve with the dipping sauce and Garlic Rice.

INGREDIENTS NOTE

Ketchap manis is a thick, dark, sweet soy sauce native to Indonesia. If you can't track it down (it's stocked by our neighbour The Spice Shop), use 3 tbsp ordinary soy sauce mixed with 1 tbsp dark brown sugar.

Lebanese cucumbers are shorter and stubbier with less pips and a sweeter, less watery flavour than the long ridged English variety. Look out for them in Greek, Lebanese and other Middle Eastern food shops.

SPICED CRISP ROAST PORK BELLY
WITH CARAMELISED PEANUT & CHILLI RELISH

Courtesy of Tom Kime comes this most succulent dish of roast belly of pork with a spiced seasoning and the crispest of crunchiest cracklings. The relish is utterly compulsive - we have been known to eat leftovers from Tom's workshops entirely unaccompanied and straight from the bowl by the spoonful!

Tom's serving suggestion is a hot and sour green mango salad, but, while fully endorsing this harmonious pairing (see page 79 in his inspirational *Exploring Taste + Flavour),* we felt you may appreciate a somewhat less challenging (in terms of shopping) but nonetheless deliciously fresh, alternative side dish. If so, see page 69 for our Crisp Salad with Chilli Lime Dressing.

SERVES 4-6

FOR THE PORK
3 tbsp coarse salt
1 tbsp coriander seeds
10 peppercorns
5 star anise
4 kaffir lime leaves
2 cinnamon sticks
$^1/_2$ tsp crushed chilli flakes
$^1/_2$ tbsp olive oil
1 $^1/_2$ kg (3 lb) boned organic pork belly in one piece, skin on and scored

FOR THE RELISH
3 tbsp olive oil
2 garlic cloves, finely chopped
1 red chilli, seeded and finely chopped
4 shallots, finely chopped
2 tsp sugar
2 tbsp peeled and unsalted peanuts
$^1/_2$ tsp ground coriander
1 tbsp sesame oil
1 tbsp soy sauce
juice 1 lime
2 tbsp chopped fresh coriander (cilantro)

Crisp Salad with Chilli Lime Dressing to serve (see page 69)

HEAT THE OVEN to 220 C (425 F) Gas 7.

Work the salt, coriander seeds and peppercorns until crushed, either by pounding with a pestle and mortar or by whizzing in a food processor. Add the star anise, lime leaves and cinnamon and continue to work until fairly finely ground. Put this spice mix in a roasting tin and pour in enough cold water to fill the tin by about 2 cm (1 inch).

Put the belly skin side down in the tin. The spiced liquid should be deep enough to submerge the skin and the first deep layer of fat – top up with more water as needed. Bring the liquid to the boil over a medium heat and simmer for 20 minutes to dissolve some of the fat. Remove from the heat, take out the belly and pour off any liquid. Rub the chilli, oil and any spice mix left in the bottom of the tin into the pork skin, then put the pork skin side up on a rack in the tin.

Roast the pork for half an hour, then turn down the oven to 180 C (350 F) Gas 4 and bake for an hour and a half, when the crackling will be irresistibly crisp and golden and the meat meltingly tender. Remove from the oven and let stand for 5 minutes before carving – this is to allow the juices to settle inside the meat.

While the meat is roasting, make the relish. Warm one tablespoon of the oil in a heavy-bottomed pan over medium high heat. Add the garlic and chilli and cook until fragrant, 1 minute. Stir in the shallots and sugar and cook, stirring, until the sugar starts to caramelise, about 2 minutes. Add in the peanuts and coriander. Cook, stirring, until the peanuts and shallots are nicely golden, about 4 minutes, adding a splash of water if the shallots start to scorch before the nuts are lightly browned, then straightaway take the pan off the heat.

Transfer the peanut mixture to a pestle and mortar and pound until crushed to coarsely ground nut butter consistency. Mix in the sesame oil, soy sauce, lime juice, coriander (cilantro) and remaining olive oil until evenly blended. Stir in enough (about two tablespoonfuls) water to make a just about drizzle-able sauce. Just before serving, warm through in a small pan over low heat.

Place the pork on a chopping board and cut into long slices about 2 cm ($^3/_4$ inch) thick. Serve at once, with the warm relish spooned over, and the crunchy salad on the side.

CUMIN LAMB & AUBERGINE STEW

A pleasingly aromatic and warming supper stew from the wondrous Lindsey Bareham's really useful *Just One Pot*. We like to add pasta too, which rather negates the one-pan thesis of the recipe, but makes for a really substantial all-in-one dish.

We've also cooked this dish to great acclaim in the test kitchen with meatballs made from the cumin and minced lamb. Put 500 g (1 lb) minced lamb, 1 chopped onion, 1 crushed garlic clove, 1 tbsp ground cumin, 2 tsp salt and a pinch of cayenne into a food processor and pulse until well mixed. Divide into 24 pieces and, with wet hands to avoid sticking, roll into balls. Follow the recipe as directed, using the cumin-spiced lamb balls instead of the cumin-coated lamb cubes.

SERVES 4

4 tbsp olive oil
2 aubergines, cut into 2 cm (³/₄ inch) cubes
2 red onions, finely chopped
4 garlic cloves, finely chopped
750 g (1 ¹/₂ lb) organic lamb shoulder, cut into 2 cm (³/₄ inch) cubes
1 tbsp ground cumin
400 g (14 oz) tin chopped Italian plum tomatoes
1 tbsp balsamic vinegar
1 garlic clove, crushed
125 ml (4 fl oz/¹/₂ cup) fresh creamy yoghurt
salt, black pepper
200 g (7 oz) risi, puntalette or other rice-shaped pasta or use any small pasta shape (optional)
1 handful fresh mint, finely chopped

HEAT THE OVEN to 160 C (325 F) Gas 3. Warm two tablespoons of the oil in a wide, heavy-bottomed pot (with a lid) over medium high heat. Stir in the aubergine cubes and cook until crisp and golden brown, 5 to 10 minutes. Scoop out of the pot and set aside. Warm the rest of the oil in the pot, add the onions and garlic and cook, stirring until softened, about 3 minutes. Add the lamb, sprinkle evenly with the cumin and cook, stirring occasionally, until well browned on all sides, about 10 minutes. Add the tomatoes and vinegar to the pot and bring to the boil. Put on the lid and put into the oven to stew slowly for 1 hour. Stir the aubergine into the pot and return to the oven to cook until the lamb and aubergine are meltingly tender, about 30 minutes.

Stir the crushed garlic into the yoghurt with a pinch of salt. Cook the pasta (if using) in plenty of boiling salted water (use the instructions on the packet as a guide but start testing a couple of minutes before the suggested time is up) until *al dente,* that is, just tender but still firm to the bite. Drain the pasta and add to the stew with most of the mint. Toss well to coat and add salt and pepper to taste. Serve at once in warmed bowls, topping each portion with a dollop of the garlic yoghurt and a scattering of fresh mint.

SPICY SAUSAGE PASTA WITH CAPERS, OLIVES & FETA

We've rather fallen in love with a splendid little book called *Sausage & Mash* by talented wine and food writer – and good friend to Books for Cooks - Fiona Beckett. This slim paperback is simply stuffed with succulent ways with sausages – all super supper solutions for the time-challenged cooks among us - plus all manner of marvellous mashes, deeply savoury gravies and other big-flavour sausage go-withs.

We use the Chicken, honey & herb sausages devised by Eric for Rosie's family farm Sheepdrove Organic Farm (see their website www.sheepdrove.com), but any really good pure meat (yes, that means no rusk, rice flour or other such sawdust) sausage will do.

As Fiona points out, bear in mind that the feta, plus the capers, olives and any seasoning in the sausages, usually contributes salt enough to the dish, so don't be tempted to add any extra to the sauce before tasting!

SERVES 4

2 tbsp olive oil
1 red onion, chopped
4 organic chicken or best pure meat sausages, skinned and crumbled
2 garlic cloves, crushed
$^1/_4$ tsp crushed chilli flakes
1 glass white wine
400 g (14 oz) tin chopped Italian plum tomatoes
2 tbsp capers, rinsed
12 green olives, stoned and roughly chopped
400 g (14 oz) penne rigate
1 handful fresh flat-leaf parsley, chopped
100 g (3 $^1/_2$ oz) feta cheese, drained and crumbled

WARM THE OIL in a large frying pan over medium high heat. Add the onion and cook until soft and just crisp around the edges, about 5 minutes. Stir in the crumbled sausage, garlic and chilli. Fry quite briskly, stirring well to break up the sausage meat, until nicely browned, 5 to 10 minutes. Pour in the wine, let it bubble up, then add the tomatoes, capers and olives. Give the sauce a good stir, adjust the heat to a steady simmer and leave to cook for 15 minutes while you turn your attention to the pasta.

Cook the pasta in plenty of boiling salted water (use the instructions on the packet as a guide but start testing a couple of minutes before the suggested time is up) until *al dente,* that is, just tender but still firm to the bite. Drain the pasta and add to the sauce with half the parsley. Toss well to coat, then spoon on to warmed plates, scatter with the feta and the rest of the parsley and serve at once.

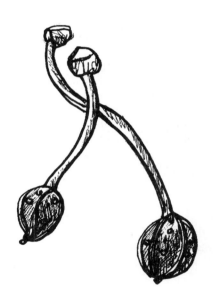

CATALAN CHICKEN WITH PRAWNS & PICADA

Books for Cooks' cook Jenny Chandler will be well known to our workshop regulars. Every couple of months she drives down from Bristol - where she runs her own cookery school The Plum Cooking Company - to give a cluster of classes with a mainly Mediterranean theme. However her true passion is the food of Spain – she has been in love with the country, culture and cuisine since her teenage years. Who better than Jenny, fluent in Catalonian, Castilian and the Spanish passion for good food, to write a Spanish cookbook – so we are thrilled to announce the arrival of *The Food of Northern Spain*!

Jenny explains how this combo of surf and turf is typically Catalan. Historically, on the Costa Brava, chicken and pork were eaten only on feast days and even then there was barely enough to feed everyone. So resourceful cooks added what they had in abundance to pad out a dish, with mussels added to stretch the rabbit a little further and, inconceivable today, lobster or prawns thrown in to so there'd be enough chicken (a special treat) to go round.

However, we think the magic ingredient of this succulent stew is unquestionably the picada - a blend of herbs, nuts, garlic, spices and crispy fried bread added to a dish just before serving. This pungent mix seasons, enriches and thickens, transforming the thin juices of any braise, casserole or stew of a vaguely Mediterranean provenance into substantial sauce brimming with flavour. A truly ab fab way to jazz up leftover stews (whether meaty or veggie) with fresh flavour, colour and texture, Jenny's picada is now firmly ensconced in our culinary bag of tricks – do try it and see why!

SERVES 4

2 tbsp olive oil
4 organic chicken thighs and 4 organic chicken drumsticks
12 large raw prawns, heads and shells on
2 onions, finely chopped
200 g (7 oz) tin Italian plum tomatoes, chopped
small glass brandy (preferably Spanish!)
1 tbsp flour
300 ml (10 fl oz/1 1/4 cups) chicken stock or water
1 bay leaf
1 tsp fresh thyme leaves or 1/2 tsp dried thyme
salt, black pepper

FOR THE PICADA
12 almonds
1 slice white bread (day-old is fine)
2 tbsp olive oil for frying, plus 4-6 tbsp to finish
3 cloves garlic
2 tbsp chopped fresh flat-leaf parsley
salt

WARM THE OIL in a wide, heavy-bottomed pan over medium-high heat and, when the oil is hot, put in the chicken and brown well on all sides. You will need to do this in batches, because, if the pan is too full, the chicken will steam rather than fry. When all the chicken pieces are nicely golden brown, set aside.

Add the prawns to the pot and cook briefly until they just turn pink, then set aside with the chicken. Turn the heat down to medium, add the onion and cook, stirring occasionally, until soft and yellow, 10 minutes. Stir in the tomatoes and let bubble down until thickened, 5 minutes. Pour in the brandy, stand well back and hold a lighted match to the side of the pan to flambé. When the flames have died down, stir the flour and, still stirring, pour over the stock or water. Adjust the heat to a slow simmer, return the chicken pieces to the pan with the bay and thyme and stew gently until the chicken is cooked through, about 25 minutes.

While the stew is simmering, make your picada. Toast the almonds in a dry frying pan over a low heat until nutty and golden on both sides, about 5 minutes. Fry the bread in hot oil until really nicely crisp and golden. Traditionally, the ingredients are pounded to a paste in a pestle and mortar, but a food processor or blender will do (you may have to scrape down the sides with a spatula once or twice). Work the almonds, fried bread, garlic and parsley until finely chopped. With the motor still running, trickle in just enough oil to make a smooth, thick paste. Add salt to taste.

Just before serving, stir in the picada and the prawns and simmer gently to heat through and allow the flavours to blend, about 5 minutes. Serve hot with good crusty bread.

THINK AHEAD
You can make the stew a day ahead, but fry up the prawns and add to the stew with the picada just before serving for maximum flavour. The picada can be made a day ahead; keep covered and chilled.

CRAB, CHILLI & LIME SCATTERED SUSHI

Scattered sushi is the easiest sushi to make – you get all the flavour of sushi with none of the fiddle faddle in a satisfying one-course meal. This splendid recipe comes from our very own Kimiko Barber's definitive book *Sushi – Taste and Technique*. For more essential sushi know-how, look no further than one of Kim's hands-on sushi workshops here at Books for Cooks.

Kim likes to serve the salad on a bed of nori seaweed; place a sheet of the seaweed on each plate and pile the crab and rice on top.

SERVES 4

FOR THE RICE
300 g (10 oz/1 1/4 cups) Japanese short grain rice
325 ml (11 fl oz/1 1/3 cups) water
4 tbsp Japanese rice vinegar
2 tbsp sugar
1/2 tsp salt

FOR THE SALAD
175 g (6 oz) fresh or frozen and defrosted crabmeat
2 fresh red chillies, seeded and finely sliced
juice 1 lime
1 handful fresh coriander (cilantro) leaves
1 lime, quartered, to garnish

PREPARE THE RICE. Put the rice in a sieve, submerge the sieve in a large bowl of water and wash the rice thoroughly. Discard the milky, starchy water, refill the bowl with fresh water and carry on washing and changing the water until it is clear. Drain and leave the rice to stand in the sieve for half an hour. Put the washed rice in a heavy pan with a lid. Pour in the water, put on the lid and bring to the boil over a medium heat. Do resist the temptation to lift the lid and peak, but listen for the sound of boiling instead. When the water boils, turn the heat up to high and boil hard for exactly 5 minutes before reducing the heat to low and simmering for another 10 minutes. Remove from the heat and leave to stand for 10 minutes.

Meanwhile, heat the vinegar, sugar and salt in a non-aluminium saucepan over low heat, stirring constantly to dissolve the sugar and salt. Don't let it boil and remove from the heat as soon as the syrup is completely clear, then leave to cool.

Put the rice in a large mixing bowl and pour a little of the vinegar syrup into the rice. Gently fold the syrup into the rice with the spatula, then spread the rice in an even layer in the bowl. Repeat until all the syrup has been added and the rice looks glossy and has cooled to room temperature.

Add the crabmeat, chillies and lime to the rice and fold in gently. To serve, heap up the salad on a single platter or divide among four plates, scatter with coriander leaves and top with lime quarters.

BRAISED LAMB WITH TAMARIND & DATES

A very, very tasty dish indeed – tender lamb braised in a dark and glossy sauce bursting with sweet and sour flavours – from Peter Gordon's *A World in Your Kitchen*. The original recipe called for lamb shanks, but we, budget-conscious as we are in the test kitchen, use shoulder. If you would like to use shanks, place six shanks in a roasting tin in a single layer and roast in a preheated 220 C (425 F) Gas 7 oven until nicely browned on all sides, about 25 minutes, then proceed as directed.

SERVES 4-6

3 tbsp sesame oil
1 kg (2 lb) organic lamb shoulder, cut into 4 cm (1 ^{1}/$_2$ inch) cubes
3 red onions, quartered
12 garlic cloves
300 ml (10 fl oz/1 ^{1}/$_4$ cups) red wine
3 carrots, grated
1 tbsp tamarind paste
1 tsp finely chopped fresh rosemary
^{1}/$_4$ tsp crushed chilli flakes
4 tbsp balsamic vinegar
4 tbsp soy sauce
250 ml (8 fl oz/1 cup) chicken or vegetable stock
250 g (8 oz/2 cups) pitted dried dates, roughly chopped
2 tbsp finely chopped fresh flat-leaf parsley

HEAT THE OVEN to 160 C (325 F) Gas 3. Warm 1 tablespoon of the oil in a wide heavy-bottomed pot (with lid) over medium heat. Add the lamb to the pot and cook until sealed and browned on all sides. You'll probably need to do this in batches because, if the pot is overcrowded, the meat will steam rather than brown. Scoop the meat out and set aside.

Warm the remaining oil in the pot. Add the onion and garlic and cook, stirring, until slightly softened, about 3 minutes. Pour in the wine and bring to the boil. Add the carrots, tamarind, rosemary, chilli, vinegar and soy and return the meat to the pot. Add just enough stock so that the level of the liquid is no higher than a couple of centimetres (about an inch) below the surface of the meat. Put on the lid and put into the oven to stew slowly until tender, about 2 hours. Add the dates, stir well and cook for another 20 minutes. Adjust the seasoning with soy and chilli, scatter with parsley and serve hot, with a nice mash (look back to our All-Purpose Mix N' Match Root Vegetable Purée in *Favourite Recipes from Books for Cooks 1, 2 & 3)* or perhaps rice or couscous, which you have buttered and herbed with fresh coriander or mint.

THINK AHEAD
Like all good stews, this braise only improves when made the day before. Cool completely before covering and chilling and reheat gently, without hard boiling – or the meat will toughen.

FILO SAUSAGE & SPINACH PIE

This easy peasy pie has become a regular feature on the Books for Cooks lunch menu. We use those shallow baking dishes with ears, but any pie or baking dish or tart tin about 15 cm (6 inches) wide and about 3 cm (1 ½ inches) deep will do.

We use the Chicken, honey and herb sausages devised by Eric for Rosie's family farm Sheepdrove Organic Farm (see their website www.sheepdrove.com), but any really good pure meat (yes, that means no rusk, rice flour or other such sawdust) sausage will do.

SERVES 4

30 g (1 oz/2 tbsp) butter
1 onion, finely chopped
4 organic chicken or best pure meat sausages, skinned and crumbled
8 garlic cloves, finely chopped
2 carrots, finely diced
200 ml (7 fl oz/⁷⁄₈ cup) crème fraîche or double (heavy) cream
180 g (6 oz) baby or young spinach leaves
salt, black pepper, freshly grated nutmeg
125 g (4 oz) filo pastry (you need 8 sheets in total)
olive oil for brushing

MELT THE BUTTER in a large frying pan over medium heat. Add the onion and cook until softened, about 5 minutes. Stir in the crumbled sausage, garlic and carrots. Fry quite briskly, stirring well to break up the sausage meat, until lightly browned, 5 to 10 minutes. Stir in the cream and warm through, but don't allow to boil. Take the pan off the heat, add the spinach and stir until wilted. Add salt, pepper and nutmeg to taste and set aside to cool slightly.

Heat the oven to 200 C (400 F) Gas 6. Brush one sheet of filo with olive oil. Fold in half and brush with little more oil. Fold and oil again. Press the filo into one of the pie dishes. Repeat with three of the remaining filo sheets. Divide the creamy sausage and spinach mixture among the pie dishes. Brush one of the remaining filo sheets with olive oil. Pick up the filo sheet with one hand (using all your fingers) just as though you were picking up a dropped handkerchief from the floor – the filo sheet will scrunch up in your fingers. Place the scrunched up filo on top of a pie. Repeat with the remaining filo and pies.

Don't fuss over making the pie tops neat – they'll look nice when baked, we promise.

Bake the pies until the filo is crisp and golden, 10-15 minutes. Serve hot – they're really a one-dish meal in themselves so no accompaniment is strictly necessary when serving as a simple supper or luncheon dish.

THINK AHEAD
You can make these pies several hours ahead and chill until ready to bake. Or you can make and bake them the day before and reheat them in a 160 C (325 F) Gas 3 oven for 20 to 25 minutes.

CARDAMOM YOGHURT CHICKEN

Sarah Benjamin (of Books for Cooks 6 renown) introduced us to this subtly spiced simple supper solution from *Stylish Indian in Minutes* by Monisha Bharadwaj and it's now a firm favourite in the Books for Cooks "everyday easy" recipe portfolio!

SERVES 4

2 tbsp sunflower oil
1 tsp ground cardamom (plus extra to finish the dish)
8 organic chicken thighs, skinned, boned and halved
1 tsp chilli powder
1 tsp ground turmeric
2 tsp tomato purée
150 ml (5 fl oz/²/₃ cup) thick creamy yoghurt
150 ml (5 fl oz/²/₃ cup) water
salt

WARM THE OIL in a large frying pan over medium high heat. Add most of the cardamom, reserving a pinch to garnish the dish, and cook until fragrant, about 1 minute. Add the chicken pieces and cook until lightly coloured on all sides, 5 to 10 minutes. Stir in the chilli, turmeric and tomato purée and cook, stirring, until the chicken is evenly coloured and the spices are fragrant, about 2 minutes. Stir in the yoghurt and water. Adjust the heat and simmer steadily until the chicken is cooked through and the sauce reduced, about 15 minutes. Season to taste with salt, sprinkle with a pinch or two of ground cardamom and serve hot with steamed basmati rice and a jar of curried chutney.

Salads & Sides

EGYPTIAN FETA SALAD WITH DILL & MINT

Jennifer's wholly essential *The Well-Dressed Salad* just flies off the shelf every time she demonstrates this dish in her salad workshop at Books for Cooks. Give it a try and you'll certainly see why.

SERVES 4

200 g (7 oz) feta cheese
3 tbsp olive oil
juice $1/2$ lemon
$1/2$ tsp black pepper
2 Lebanese cucumbers, trimmed and diced, or 1 medium cucumber, de-seeded
    and diced
1 small red onion, finely chopped
2 tbsp chopped fresh mint
2 tbsp chopped fresh dill
2 tbsp chopped fresh flat-leaf parsley
salt

Crumble the feta into a bowl and mash with the oil and lemon juice. Season to taste with the black pepper. Add the cucumber, onion, mint, dill and parsley and mix gently to evenly combine. Taste and add salt if necessary (the feta can be salty enough).

THINK AHEAD
You can chop all the vegetables and mash the feta up to 3 hours in advance, but do not assemble the salad until just before serving.

PUMPKIN WITH FIVE SPICES

From Monisha Bharadwaj's *Stylish Indian in Minutes* comes this brightly coloured and flavoured dish of orange pumpkin cubed, caramelized and coated with toasted spices. It makes an unusual and lively accompaniment for grilled chicken or lamb, but can be elevated to light meal status by serving with steamed rice, thick creamy yoghurt and a scattering of fresh coriander (cilantro) leaves.

SERVES 4

800 g (1 lb 10 oz) orange-fleshed pumpkin or butternut squash, cut in 3 cm
    (1¹/₄ inch) cubes with skin
2 tbsp sunflower or olive oil
¹/₂ tsp cumin seeds
¹/₂ tsp fennel seeds
¹/₂ tsp fenugreek seeds
¹/₂ tsp brown or black mustard seeds
¹/₂ tsp black onion seeds
1 tsp sugar
1 tsp salt
a pinch of cayenne

WARM THE OIL in a large frying pan over high heat. Add cumin, fennel, fenugreek, mustard and onion seeds and cook until the seeds pop, 1 to 2 minutes. Add the pumpkin, sugar, salt and cayenne, stir well to coat each cube with the seeds, and cook, stirring frequently, until the pumpkin is tender and slightly caramelized, which will take anywhere from 10 to 15 minutes, depending on the ripeness of your pumpkin. Adjust the seasoning with salt and cayenne and serve immediately.

FARRO & ROAST TOMATO SALAD
WITH ANCHOVY, MINT & PECORINO DRESSING

Yes, another recipe using farro *aka* spelt – see also page 14 and Ursula's Farro and Borlotti Soup. As we explained before, we are increasingly asked for recipes that use farro or spelt - in fact one Saturday, three customers requested farro/spelt recipes in a row! Our little books have a modest tradition of promoting all kinds of ingredients, some new and exotic, some traditional and fallen from favour – pomegranate molasses, chipotles in adobo and mutton to name a few. Well, this year it's the turn of this ancient grain to step into the culinary spotlight.

Look out for farro and spelt in delis, health food shops and Italian stores, but if you can't track either down, you can also use wheat (sometimes called wheat berries), kamut (another ancient grain) or pearl barley (our preference) instead since they all have a nuttiness of flavour in common. Farro and spelt take about 1 1/2 to 2 hours to cook until tender. Alternatively, you can soak the grains overnight and they'll be ready in about half the time.

This salad of Jennifer's can be found in her sensational *Small Bites*. We find it's punchy flavours set off the chewy texture and nutty taste of these great grains to perfection. Vegetarians don't have to miss out - they need only omit the anchovy for a veggie-friendly salad.

SERVES 4

FOR THE SALAD
250 g (8 oz/1 cup) farro or spelt, soaked overnight
250 g (8 oz) ripe cherry tomatoes, halved
2 tbsp olive oil
salt, black pepper
1 red onion, finely chopped
juice of 1/2 lemon
3 celery stalks, finely sliced
60 g (2 oz) Pecorino, coarsely grated (use the large holes on your grater)
4 tbsp raisins, soaked in warm water for 10 minutes, then drained
3 tbsp roughly chopped fresh mint
2 tbsp roughly chopped fresh basil
2 tbsp roughly chopped fresh flat-leaf parsley

FOR THE DRESSING
6 tbsp olive oil
1 garlic clove, finely chopped
1 anchovy, rinsed and chopped
4 tbsp red wine vinegar
1 tsp runny honey

COOK THE FARRO in a large pan of boiling salted water until tender, about 45 minutes.

Roast the tomatoes while the farro is cooking. Heat the oven to 180 C (350 F) Gas 4. Place the tomatoes in a baking tray, drizzle over the oil, sprinkle with a couple of pinches each salt and pepper and mix to evenly coat the tomato halves with oil and seasoning, then bake until softened and slightly wilted, about 25 minutes.

Meanwhile, put the onion with the lemon juice in a large mixing bowl and let stand for 10 minutes – this lemon-marinating makes the onion less aggressively raw onion-y. When the farro is tender, drain and stir at once into the lemon-y onion.

Make the dressing. Warm the oil in a small frying pan over low heat, add the garlic and anchovy and cook until the garlic is lightly golden and the anchovy melting, about 3 minutes. Remove from the heat and stir in the vinegar and honey. Add salt and pepper to taste, then pour over the farro and mix well to coat the grains.

Gently fold in the celery, pecorino, raisins, roast tomatoes, mint, basil and parsley into the farro until evenly combined. Adjust the seasoning, adding salt, pepper, vinegar and oil as needed. To serve, pile on to individual plates or a large platter. Best served at room temperature.

THINK AHEAD
You can make and dress the salad up to 2 hours in advance but the fresh herbs are best added not long before serving.

BUTTERED SPICED LENTILS

A really luscious dal, creamy, buttery and fragrantly spiced, from Manju Malhi's *Indian with Passion*. You'll probably need access to an Indian or Asian food shop to track down black lentils, also called black gram (but sometimes labelled urd or urad); be sure to buy the whole not split lentils.

But don't miss out on this spicy bean stew just because you don't have the authentic pulse. You could use just red kidney beans, which already feature in the dal, or, if you want to stick to the original colour scheme, a mix of black and red beans – turn to Spicy Braised Oxtail on page 40 for instructions on cooking red beans or use tinned. Serve as an accompaniment to grilled lamb or as a meal in its own right with steamed rice and thick creamy yoghurt.

SERVES 4

175 g (6 oz/³/₄ cup) whole black lentils, soaked overnight
100 g (3 ¹/₂ oz/7 tbsp) butter
asafoetida (optional – see ingredients note below)
1 onion, finely chopped
2 fresh green chillies, seeded and finely chopped
4 garlic cloves, finely chopped
2 cm (³/₄ inch) fresh ginger, grated
¹/₂ tsp turmeric
¹/₄ tsp chilli powder
1 ¹/₂ tsp ground coriander
1 tsp ground cumin
1 – 400 g (14 oz) tin red kidney beans, drained and rinsed
salt
¹/₄ tsp garam masala
3 tbsp double (heavy) cream
1 handful coriander (cilantro) leaves, roughly chopped

Drain and rinse the lentils, put in a large pan (with a lid), cover with fresh water by at least 2 cm (1 inch) and bring to a boil. Boil hard for 5 minutes, then put on the lid, adjust the heat to a steady simmer and cook until tender, about half an hour.

Melt half the butter in a pot over medium heat. Add a pinch of asafoetida, if using, onion, fresh chilli and garlic and cook, stirring once or twice, until the onion is soft and lightly golden, 5 to 10 minutes. Add the ginger, turmeric, chilli powder, ground coriander and cumin and cook until fragrant, 1 minute. Stir in the lentils and beans, add enough lentil cooking liquor to come just level with, but not submerge, the pulses and simmer steadily for 15 minutes. Adjust the seasoning, adding salt and chilli to taste. Spoon into a warmed serving dish, sprinkle over the garam masala and dot with the remaining butter. Swirl over the cream and sprinkle with coriander. Serve at once.

INGREDIENTS NOTE
Asafoetida is the dried and ground root of the giant fennel plant. It's much used in Indian cookery to flavour pulse dishes – as well as to combat their flatulent effects!

THINK AHEAD
You can make this spicy lentil and bean stew a day or two ahead of time, but finish with the butter, garam masala, cream and fresh coriander just before serving.

SOFT POLENTA

Annabel Langbein chooses soft polenta to accompany her superlative Spicy Braised Oxtail (see page 40) but you could also try serving with the Spicy Sausage Sauce on page 57 of *Favourite Recipes from Books for Cooks 1, 2 & 3* or the Gorgonzola Sauce on page 30 of this little book.

You can jazz up this basic recipe with all sorts of flavoursome additions – cheese (think grated Parmesan or Pecorino, crumbled Gorgonzola, cubed Taleggio), roast garlic, chopped fresh rosemary or oregano, sliced black olives or crème fraîche. Any leftover polenta can be sliced, then brushed with olive oil and grilled or fried in butter until crisp and golden.

SERVES 4

1 ¼ litres (2 pints/5 cups) water
1 tsp salt
175 g (6 oz/1 cup) polenta or cornmeal
30 g (1 oz/¼ stick) butter
black pepper

HEAT THE OVEN TO 180 C (350 F) Gas 4. Bring the water to a boil in a heavy-bottomed pan and add the salt. Adjust the heat to a steady simmer.

Put the polenta in jug and slowly pour in a thin and steady stream into the simmering water while the other hand stirs constantly with a whisk to stop any lumps forming.

When smoothly combined, cover the pan with a lid, put into the oven and bake until thick and soft, 25 to 30 minutes.

Alternatively, if you want to cook the polenta the authentically Italian way, turn the heat down as low as possible and cook, stirring occasionally with a wooden spoon, until thick and soft, 25 to 30 minutes. You may want to cover your hand with a tea towel when you stir because the polenta tends to spit volcanically as it bubbles.

Remove from the heat and beat in the butter. Adjust the seasoning and serve at once.

CRISP SALAD WITH CHILLI LIME DRESSING

Most oriental vegetable salads involve lots of fine slicing and neat dicing – too much knife work, perhaps, for the time-challenged cook – so we thought you might appreciate this chunky, crunchy salad as a less onerous alternative. Pair this refreshingly zesty side with Tom's Spiced Crisp Roast Pork (see page 46) and other such Asian dishes.

SERVES 4

FOR THE DRESSING
6 tbsp lime juice
2 tbsp Thai fish sauce
2 tsp sugar
1 fresh red chilli, seeded and finely chopped

FOR THE SALAD
1 cucumber, unpeeled
3 little gem or baby cos (romaine) lettuces
2 tbsp fresh mint leaves
2 spring onions, finely sliced

MAKE THE DRESSING. Mix together the lime, fish sauce, sugar and chilli until the sugar has dissolved.

Cut the cucumbers in quarter lengthways. Cut each quarter across into three lengths, slightly on the diagonal. Cut each lettuce into quarters lengthways. Place the cucumber and lettuce wedges in a large mixing bowl. Just before serving, pour over the dressing and mix well. Pile on to a serving dish, scatter with mint and spring onions and serve at once.

AUBERGINES IN SPICY HONEY SAUCE

We owe the entry of this truly heavenly dish from Claudia Roden's sublime *Tamarind and Saffron* into the Books for Cooks repertoire to Victoria Blashford Snell, co-author of *Books for Cooks 1, 2 & 3* and *4, 5 & 6*. Victoria's now far too in demand as a successful caterer to have any spare time over to cook at Books for Cooks, but she still finds time for many Books for Cooks get-togethers where her cooking and Sherlock Holmesian nose for a great recipe continue to impress. It makes a splendid starter or luscious light lunch served with warm flat bread or succulent side dish to accompany roast or grilled lamb.

Don't be tempted to skip peeling the aubergines as the skin remains tough and spoils the meltingly tender texture of this sublime, sweetly spicy dish.

SERVES 4

2 medium aubergines
olive oil
salt

FOR THE SAUCE
2 tbsp olive oil
3 garlic cloves, crushed
5 cm (2 inch) piece fresh ginger, grated
1 ^{1}/$_2$ tsp ground cumin
a pinch of cayenne
6 tbsp runny honey
juice 1 lemon
150 ml (5 fl oz/^{2}/$_3$ cup) water

PEEL THE AUBERGINES and cut across into 1 cm (^{1}/$_2$ inch) thick slices.

Pour some olive oil into a shallow dish and dip the peeled aubergine rounds into the oil on both sides. Grill on a barbecue, under an overhead grill or on a ridged cast-iron grill pan until golden brown, about 3 minutes on each side. Sprinkle the slices with salt as you turn them so they're salted on both sides. The aubergine slices don't need to be tender as they'll finish cooking in the sauce, so the grilling is more a question of colour and flavour than doneness.

Warm the oil in a large frying pan over low heat. Add the garlic and cook until fragrant, about 1 minute, then stir in the ginger, cumin, cayenne, honey, lemon juice and water.

Gently stir in the aubergine rounds, making sure that each round is well coated with the sauce. Simmer slowly until the aubergines are tender and have imbued most of the sauce, about 10 minutes. Remove from the heat and check the seasoning, adding more salt and cayenne as needed. Serve while still just warm or at room temperature.

RED PEPPER BULGUR

This lovely side dish of nutty bulgur, smoky peppers and fragrant fresh herbs comes from the Sams Clark and their *Casa Moro*. We like to serve this grainy salad with roast or grilled lamb but it also nicely completes a mezze table or buffet spread. If you don't have any hot paprika, use sweet instead but add a pinch of cayenne (or to taste) to compensate.

SERVES 4

3 red peppers
175 g (6 oz/1 cup) medium or coarse bulgur
6 spring onions, finely sliced
2 garlic cloves, crushed
$^1/_2$ tsp hot paprika
1 tbsp tomato purée
3 tbsp olive oil
2 tbsp roughly chopped fresh flat-leaf parsley
2 tbsp roughly chopped fresh mint
1 tbsp roughly chopped fresh dill (if you can find it)
salt, black pepper
3 handfuls baby gem or cos (romaine) lettuce leaves

GRILL THE PEPPERS either under a preheated overhead grill (good), or over the naked flame of a gas hob (better), or on a barbecue (best) and cook, turning, until evenly charred and blistered all over. Put the peppers in a bowl, cover with a plate, and leave for 10 minutes while the trapped steam loosens the pepper skins so they may easily be slipped off. Then peel, core and seed the peppers before very finely chopping to a semi-purée.

Soak the bulgur in warm water for 15 minutes, then squeeze dry and put in a large mixing bowl with the chopped peppers, spring onions, garlic, paprika, tomato puree, olive oil and fresh herbs. Mix everything well together and add salt and pepper to taste. To serve, heap up the red pepper bulgur on a bed of the salad leaves.

THINK AHEAD
You can make this salad a day in advance. Cover and chill but add the spring onions and herbs no more than an hour or so before serving.

GARLIC RICE

We think this method produces perfectly streamed fluffy rice - and it's basically foolproof. It's more the "scant-two-to-one" method than the classic "two-to-one" method as we find the latter makes for just a little too much liquid for the rice to absorb for perfect doneness.

SERVES 4

2 tbsp sunflower or olive oil
3 garlic cloves, sliced
250 ml (8 fl oz/1 cup) basmati rice, soaked in cold water for 30 minutes
   (if you're short of time, rinse well under the cold tap)
1/4 tsp salt
225 ml (9 fl oz/7/8 cup) chicken, vegetable stock or water

Warm the oil in a heavy-bottomed pan (with a lid) over medium high heat. Add the garlic and stir-fry until golden and fragrant, about 3 minutes. Stir in the rice and cook, stirring, until each grain is coated with the oil, about 1 minute. Add the salt and ladle in the stock. Bring to the boil, adjust the heat so that liquid simmers and cook for no longer than 8 minutes. Put on the lid, turn off the heat and leave for 20 minutes, then fluff up with a fork and serve hot.

HERBED RICE
Use 1 finely chopped shallot or 3 finely chopped spring onions (scallions) instead of the garlic and stir-fry until softened, 3 to 5 minutes. Add the rice with a bay leaf and cook as directed. To finish, stir a couple of tablespoons of the finely chopped fresh leafy herb of your choice (flat-leaf parsley, coriander (cilantro), basil, chives, marjoram, dill or chervil, for instance) or 1/2 tsp finely chopped woody herb – (such as thyme or rosemary) or a mixture into the rice.

THINK AHEAD
If you're not ready to eat, you can leave the rice, covered with the lid, standing for up to 30 minutes before serving. Alternatively, transfer to a low oven (plate warming temperature really) where it will be fine for an hour or so.

HORSERADISH & BREAD SAUCE

Every year we invite all Books for Cooks staff past and present to a get-together at the shop and it was at one of our summer parties that we first tasted this splendid variation on horseradish relish. We straightaway begged the recipe from the cook who had produced our party feast, Tom Kime – a talented chef well-known to our workshop customers. So we were delighted to note its inclusion in Tom's first cookbook *Exploring Taste + Flavour.* Thick, creamy and piquant, it makes an unusual but harmonious accompaniment to roast beef, grilled steak or homemade pure meat beef burgers.

3 slices dry day-old white bread, crusts cut off and discarded
4 1/2 tbsp milk
2 tbsp red wine vinegar
1 garlic clove, crushed
2 tbsp grated hot horseradish (fresh or from a jar)
100 ml (3 1/2 fl oz/1/3 cup + 2 tbsp) olive oil
juice 1 lemon
salt, black pepper
2 tbsp finely chopped flat-leaf parsley (optional)

PUT THE BREAD in a bowl, pour over the milk and vinegar and leave for 5 minutes to soften. Squeeze out any milky liquid from the bread and set aside. Put the bread, garlic and horseradish in a food processor and pulse to combine. With the motor running, trickle in enough of the milky soaking liquid to make a thick paste. With the motor still running, pour in the oil in a thin stream until absorbed and well blended, then add the lemon. Add salt and pepper to taste. Stir in the parsley (if using) just before serving, or the vinegar will spoil the herb's fresh green colour.

THINK AHEAD
The sauce can be made a day ahead but be sure to add the parsley not long before serving; keep covered and chilled.

Sweet things

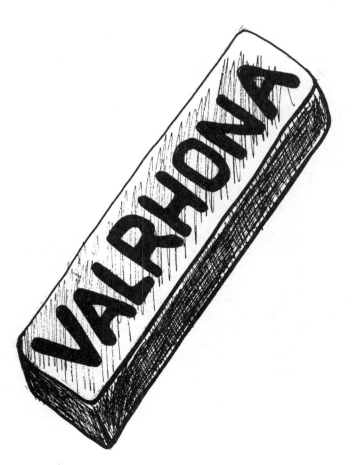

CHOCOLATE MERINGUE CAKE

One of the big hits of *Books for Cooks 5*, Olivia's Orange Meringue Cake remains a regular feature on the Test Kitchen counter, so we thought you'd definitely appreciate this doubly chocolate (choc-y meringue topping choc-y cake) version.

SERVES 8

FOR THE CAKE
150 g (5 oz/1 cup + 2 tbsp) plain (all-purpose) flour
60 g (2 oz/¹/₂ cup) cocoa powder
2 tsp baking powder
salt
125 g (4 oz/1 stick) butter, softened
125 g (4 oz/²/₃ cup) caster (granulated) sugar
1 tsp natural vanilla extract
4 organic egg yolks
275 ml (9 fl oz/1 cup + 2 tbsp) sour cream

FOR THE MERINGUE
4 organic egg whites
salt
150 g (5 oz/1 cup) icing (powdered) sugar, sifted
2 tbsp cocoa powder, sifted

HEAT THE OVEN to 160 C (325 F) Gas 3 (electric fan-assisted ovens should be set at 150 C). Butter a 24 cm (9 ¹/₂ inch) springform cake tin and line the base with baking parchment.

Make the cake. Sift the flour, cocoa, baking powder and a pinch of salt. Beat the butter, sugar and vanilla together until white and fluffy. Beat in the egg yolks one by one. Add about one-third of the flour mixture to the creamed mixture and fold in. Add one-third of the sour cream and fold in. Alternately add the remaining flour mixture and sour cream until evenly combined. Spread the cake mixture in the prepared cake tin. Set aside while you make the meringue.

Put the egg whites in a large, clean, grease-free bowl with a pinch of salt and sugar, a tablespoon at a time, whisking well after each addition, and continue whisking until the egg whites are stiff and glossy. Fold in the cocoa powder until evenly combined. Spoon the meringue in an even layer over the cake mixture.

Place on a rack in the lower half of the oven (this is because the cake rises up quite alarmingly during baking.) Bake until the meringue topping is crisp and a skewer inserted into the cake comes out clean, about 1 hour.

Transfer to a wire rack and leave to cool completely in its tin. Run a knife around the sides of the cake to loosen before unmoulding. Use a palate knife or spatula to ease the cake off the tin base to a serving dish. Serve with a spoonful of thick creamy yoghurt and, when in season, a handful of summer berries.

PLUM, LEMON & COCONUT CAKE

Lightly lemony, lusciously moist and sumptuously crowned with a ring of red plums, this splendid sweet confection hails from New Zealand's veritable queen of cakes, Julie Le Clerc. We found it in her wonderful *Café@Home* where she also imparts this invaluable tip "my advice... for best results, pour hot syrup over a cold cake or cold syrup over a hot cake so that the cake absorbs the syrup without becoming sodden." Thank you Julie!

SERVES 8

FOR THE CAKE
175 g (6 oz/1 ¹/₂ sticks) butter, softened
175 g (6 oz/³/₄ cup) caster (granulated) sugar
3 organic eggs
175 g (6 oz/1 ¹/₄ cups) plain (all-purpose) flour
150 g (5 oz/1 ¹/₂ cups) desiccated (shredded dry) coconut
2 tsp baking powder
grated zest 3 organic lemons (wash and scrub well if not organic)
5 small or 4 large red plums, cut in half

FOR THE SYRUP
200 g (7 oz/1 cup) caster (granulated) sugar
100 ml (3 ¹/₂ fl oz/¹/₃ cup + 2 tbsp) water
juice 3 lemons

HEAT THE OVEN to 180 C (350 F) Gas 4 (electric fan-assisted ovens should be set to 170 C). Butter a 24 cm (9 ¹/₂ inch) springform cake tin and line the base with baking parchment.

Beat the butter and sugar together until light and fluffy. Beat in the eggs one at a time, sprinkling in one tablespoon of the flour after each egg (this is to stop curdling). Gently fold in the remaining flour, coconut, baking powder and lemon zest. Spread the mixture evenly over the base of the prepared tin. Arrange the plum halves cut side down, skin side up over the mixture – don't push them in, just place them lightly on top because the mixture will rise as the cake bakes and you don't want the plums completely submerged in sponge. Bake until the sides of the cake have shrunk slightly away from the tin and a skewer inserted into the cake comes out clean, about 1 hour.

Make the syrup while the cake is baking. Place the sugar and water in a pan over medium heat and stir until the sugar dissolves to a clear syrup. Raise the heat, bring to the boil and simmer for 2 minutes. Remove from the heat, cool slightly, then add the lemon juice.

Take the cake from the oven and place on a wire rack (with a plate underneath to catch any escaping drips) but do not turn out. Straightaway pour the syrup over the hot cake and leave to stand until all the syrup has been soaked up, about 2 minutes. Run a knife round the sides of the cake to loosen, unmould and leave to cool completely. Dust lavishly with icing sugar before serving warm or at room temperature, with or without thick creamy yoghurt.

THINK AHEAD
This moist and sticky cake can certainly be made a day ahead; cool completely before storing at room temperature in an airtight container.

ESPRESSO CARAMEL CAKE

Coffee, caramel, hazelnuts and chocolate – what more could you desire in a dessert? This winning quartet of flavours comes from our very own Maddie Hatton, former Books for Cooks bookseller, sometime test kitchen cook and baker extraordinaire.

SERVES 8

250 g (8 oz/2 sticks) butter
250 g (8 oz/1 cup) caster (granulated) sugar
4 organic eggs
250 g (8 oz/2 cups) plain (all-purpose flour)
2 tsp baking powder
salt
200 g (7 oz/1 $1/2$ cups) chopped hazelnuts
200 g (7 oz) dark (bittersweet) chocolate, coarsely chopped

FOR THE SYRUP
150 g (5 oz/$2/3$ cup) caster (granulated) sugar
4 tbsp water
4 tbsp freshly brewed strong coffee
30 g (1 oz/2 tbsp) butter

HEAT THE OVEN to 180 C (350 F) Gas 4 (electric fan-assisted ovens should be set to 170 C). Butter a 24 cm (9 $1/2$ inch) springform cake tin and line the base with baking parchment.

Beat the butter and sugar together until light and fluffy. Beat in the eggs one at a time, sprinkling in one tablespoon of the flour after each egg (this is to stop curdling). Gently fold in the remaining flour, baking powder and a pinch of salt. Sprinkle over the chopped nuts and chocolate and gently fold in until evenly distributed throughout the cake mix. Spread the mixture evenly over the base of the prepared tin. Bake until the sides of the cake have shrunk slightly away from the tin and a skewer inserted into the cake comes out clean, about 1 hour.

Make the syrup while the cake is baking. Place the sugar and water in a heavy-bottomed pan over medium heat and stir until the sugar dissolves. Raise the heat, bring to the boil and simmer until the sugar turns a dark golden brown. Take off the heat and straightaway add the coffee and butter – stand well back as the caramel spits viciously! Stir until smoothly combined.

Take the cake from the oven and place on a wire rack (with a plate underneath to catch any escaping drips). Leave for half an hour to cool slightly, then pour the syrup over the cake. When all the syrup has been absorbed, run a knife round the sides of the cake to loosen, then turn out and leave to cool completely on the wire rack. Serve with thick cream.

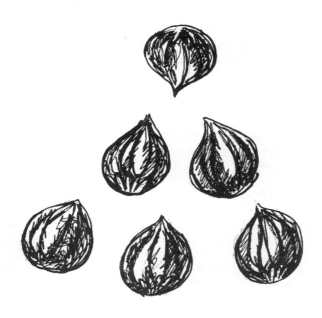

CRANBERRY TORTE WITH BUTTERSCOTCH SAUCE

Celia has a talent for sweet things. A slice of her Chocolate Banana Mascarpone Cheesecake rates as one of the great all-time dessert experiences (for the recipe, look no further than her gorgeous second cookbook *New Vegetarian*). Now here is another fabulous dessert creation, this time from her glorious *Entertaining Vegetarians*.

We have also baked this torte to great acclaim with mixed frozen berries, but, as the berries are less sharp than cranberries, we restrict the sugar for coating the berries to four tablespoons. Also you might like to ring the changes with the nuts too – instead of this classic all-American combo of cranberries and pecans, try chopped hazelnuts, almonds or walnuts.

SERVES 8

FOR THE BERRIES
500 g (1 lb) cranberries (fresh or frozen)
150 g (5 oz/1 cup) chopped pecans
100 g (3 $^1/_2$ oz/$^1/_2$ cup) caster (granulated) sugar

FOR THE BATTER
125 g (4 oz/$^1/_2$ cup) caster (granulated) sugar
1 organic egg, beaten
60 g (2 oz/$^1/_2$ cup) plain (all-purpose) flour, sifted
90 g (3 oz/$^3/_4$ stick) butter, melted
1 tsp ground cardamom

FOR THE SAUCE
175 g (6 oz/$^3/_4$ cup dark brown sugar
125 g (4 oz/1 stick) butter
125 ml (4 fl oz/$^1/_2$ cup) double (heavy) cream

HEAT OVEN TO 180 C (350 F) Gas 4 (electric fan-assisted ovens should be set to 170 C). Butter a 24 cm (9 $^1/_2$ inch) springform cake tin and line the base with baking parchment.

Prepare the berries. Place the cranberries in the tin, then sprinkle with the pecans and the sugar and mix well so the cranberries are evenly coated with sugar and nuts.

Make the batter. Reserve 2 tbsp of the sugar for sprinkling. Beat the remaining sugar with the egg in a bowl until well combined. Fold in the flour, butter and cardamom to make a smooth batter and pour over the cranberries in the tin. Sprinkle evenly with the reserved sugar and bake until firm and golden, about 45 minutes. Transfer to a wire rack and leave to cool for 30 minutes before unmoulding. Run a knife around the sides before turning out.

Make the sauce. Put the sugar, butter and cream in a small pan over a gentle heat and stir until the sugar has dissolved and the sauce is bubbling.

Serve the torte warm or at room temperature with the warm sticky sauce.

83

LEMON CURD CAKE

We make no apologies for including this citrus-scented and airily light sponge sandwiched with luscious lemon cream from *The Ultimate Cake Book*. It's true that we did feature this essential cookbook (yes, every household should have one) in our first little book, but, as the saying goes, you can't have too much of a good thing.

If Maida Heatter is America's queen of cakes, Mary Berry unquestionably reigns supreme over British baking and to Marilou, at whose insistence we included this gorgeous gateau, she is quite simply cake god. If you don't already possess a copy, this recipe represents her heartfelt plea that you buy one now!

SERVES 8

FOR THE CAKE
4 organic eggs, separated
150 g (5 oz/²/₃ cup) caster (granulated) sugar
grated zest and juice 1 lemon
75 g (2 ¹/₂ oz/³/₈ cup) semolina
20 g (³/₄ oz/3 tbsp) ground almonds
salt
icing sugar to decorate

FOR THE FILLING
175 ml (6 fl oz/³/₄ cup) double (heavy) cream
8 tbsp lemon curd
100 g (3 ¹/₂ oz) raspberries or redcurrants (optional)

HEAT THE OVEN to 180 C (350 F) Gas 4 (electric fan-assisted ovens should be set to 170 C). Butter a 24 cm (9 ¹/₂ inch) springform cake tin and line the base with baking parchment.

Whisk the egg yolks and sugar together until thick, pale and mousse-like. Gently beat in the lemon juice. Add the semolina, almonds and zest and gently fold in until evenly mixed.

Put the egg whites in a large, clean, grease-free bowl with a pinch of salt and whisk until they hold soft, slightly drooping peaks. Gently fold the beaten whites into the cake mix until evenly blended.

Spread the mixture evenly over the base of the prepared tin. Bake until the sides of the cake have shrunk slightly away from the tin and a skewer inserted into the cake comes out clean, about 45 minutes.

Take the cake from the oven and place on a wire rack. Leave for 5 minutes to cool slightly, then turn out and leave to cool completely on the wire rack.

With a serrated knife cut the cake in half horizontally, holding your hand firmly on top of the cake to guide the knife. Whisk the cream until it holds it shape, then fold in the lemon curd. Place the bottom layer of the cake on a serving dish, spread evenly with lemon cream and, if using, scatter the berries on top. Sit the other cake half on top and dust lavishly with icing sugar before serving.

INGREDIENTS NOTE

If you'd like to make your own lemon curd for this cake, put 150 ml (5 fl oz/ 2/3 cup) lemon juice, one teaspoonful grated lemon zest, 4 tbsp sugar and 60 g (2 oz/1/2 stick) butter in a small pan over low heat. Stir occasionally until the butter has melted. Beat an egg until frothy in a bowl. Continue to whisk constantly while pouring in the hot lemon butter until well blended. Return the mixture to the pan and cook over a low heat, stirring constantly, until thick and creamy, about 10 minutes. Take from the heat and keep stirring until slightly cooled, then set aside to cool completely.

If you don't fancy making your own, pick a good brand – Duchy Originals makes a super organic Traditional Lemon Curd.

ERIC'S RED WINE & CHOCOLATE CAKE

You might be forgiven for thinking that a cake combining chocolate and wine is somewhat eccentric, especially since wine buffs often maintain that pairing wine with chocolate is a no-no. However, Eric happens to be a red wine with chocolate fan, especially when it's a splendidly dark chunk of organic chocolate courtesy of Green & Black alongside a glass of his own Domaine des Savarines. It was this favourite combination that gave rise to this gorgeous gateau – indeed, when you think about red wine's red berry flavours, this is not such an outlandish marriage of flavours after all.

SERVES 8

150 ml (5 fl oz/²/₃ cup + 2 tbsp) red wine
160 g (5 ¹/₂ oz/³/₄ cup) caster (granulated sugar)
300 g (10 oz) dark (bittersweet) chocolate, broken into pieces
150 g (5 oz/1 ¹/₄ sticks) butter
5 organic eggs

HEAT OVEN TO 180 C (350 F) Gas 4 (electric fan-assisted ovens should be set to 170 C). Butter a 24 cm (9 ¹/₂ inch) springform cake tin and line the base with baking parchment.

Place the wine and sugar in a small pan over a low heat. Stir constantly to dissolve the sugar to make a clear syrup and remove from the heat just when liquid starts to tremble. Set aside to cool slightly.

Melt the butter, chocolate and half the syrup together over a very low heat and stir until smooth.

Whisk the eggs and the remaining syrup until very thick, pale and mousse-like – the mixture should hold a ribbon trail when the whisk is lifted, which will take anywhere from 5 to 10 minutes. If your electric beater is not powerful enough, or you are whisking by hand, and the whole thing is taking ages, set the bowl of eggs and sugar over a pan of hot, but definitely not boiling, water. The mixture will then mousse without tears.

Gently fold the chocolate mixture into the egg mixture until evenly combined, with no streaks of chocolate. Pour the mixture into the prepared tin, put into the oven and bake for just 20 minutes when the cake will look just set but still wobbly and moussy in the middle. Transfer to a wire rack and leave to cool completely before turning out – the eggs and chocolate will set the cake as it cools.

INGREDIENTS NOTE

The wine that inspired this cake comes from Eric's own vineyard, Le Domaine des Savarines in South West France. Medium-bodied, with subtle spice, soft tannins and forest fruit flavours, it's available by the glass or by the bottle at Books for Cooks. Alternatively, choose a red wine that's rich and fruity but not overtly oaky.

THINK AHEAD

You can make this cake up to a day ahead; store in an airtight container at room temperature.

CINNAMON SWIRL SOUR CREAM CAKE

A marginally modified and slightly scaled down version of Maida Heatter's legendary Budapest Coffee Cake, world-renowned as one of the great gateaux of all time. Marilou bakes it on a weekly basis and her interpretation of this superlative sweet treat with its moist and tender sour cream crumb and swirls of nutty chocolate sweet spice mix has had customers literally begging for the recipe. Here it is, at last!

SERVES 8

FOR THE MIX
100 g (3 ¹/₂ oz/1 cup) walnuts or pecans
4 tbsp raisins
1 tbsp ground cinnamon
1 ¹/₂ tbsp cocoa powder
175 g (6 oz/³/₄ cup) dark brown sugar

FOR THE CAKE
250 g (8 oz/2 cups) plain (all-purpose flour)
2 tsp baking powder
salt
125 g (4 oz/1 stick) butter, softened
225 g (7 ¹/₂ oz/1 scant cup) caster (granulated) sugar
1 tsp natural vanilla extract
3 organic eggs
250 ml (8 fl oz/1 cup) sour cream

Heat the oven to 180 C (350 C) Gas 4 (electric fan-assisted ovens should be set to 170 C). Butter a 24 cm (9 ¹/₂ inch) springform cake tin and line the base with baking parchment.

Make the spiced mix. Put the nuts and raisins in food processor and pulse until finely chopped. Transfer to a bowl, add the cinnamon, cocoa and sugar and mix until well combined.

Make the cake. Sift the flour, baking powder and a pinch of salt. In a separate bowl, beat the butter, sugar and vanilla together until light and fluffy. Beat in the eggs one at a time, sprinkling in one tablespoon of the flour after each egg (this is to stop curdling). Add one-third of the flour to the creamed mixture and fold in. Add one-third of the sour cream and fold in. Alternately add the remaining flour and sour cream until evenly combined.

Spread one-third of the cake mixture in a thin layer over the base of the prepared tin. Sprinkle evenly with half of the filling. Continue to layer the remaining cake mixture and filling, dropping the cake mixture in small spoonfuls evenly over the spice filling and then lightly spreading out with the back of the spoon, ending with a layer of the cake mixture. This layering is definitely easier if you divide the cake mixture into three equal-sized parts so you can be sure to have some cake mixture to make a final layer! Rap the tin on a hard surface several times to expel any air bubbles.

Bake until the sides of the cake have shrunk slightly away from the tin and a skewer inserted into the cake comes out clean, about 1 hour. Transfer to a wire rack and leave to cool for 15 minutes. Run a knife round the sides of the cake to loosen before turning out. You can serve the cake warm or at room temperature, with or without thick cream.

INGREDIENTS NOTE

Unless fresh from a newly bought pack, dark brown (*aka* muscovado or barbados sugar) is often rock hard and impossible to work with. Just in case you don't know, here's how you soften it. Take two bowls, one smaller than the other. Put the sugar in the small bowl and put the small bowl inside the big one. Pour a little hot water into the big bowl and cover with a damp tea towel. Leave for a quarter of an hour, when the sugar will be lovely and soft.

THINK AHEAD

You can make this cake a day ahead; cool completely before storing at room temperature in an airtight container.

BANOFFEE PIE

Banoffee, bannoffee, banoffie, banoffy, banoffi – we like banoffee, as it most succinctly expresses what this wicked pudding is all about: banana + toffee = ban-offee. But, to be pedantic, this legendary pie was in fact christened "banoffi" when it appeared on the menus of the Hungry Monk restaurant in Jevington, East Sussex, in the early seventies. The original recipe, which first appeared in print in *The Deeper Secrets of the Hungry Monk* in 1974, called for shortcrust pastry, but we have come to prefer a cheesecake-style crushed biscuit crust. We are rather partial to gingernuts, but do feel free to use whatever flavour and brand you fancy to make your crust – if you do care to recreate an authentic pie, simple turn to pages 104-6 and follow our instructions for making shortcrust pastry. Interestingly, two of the cookbooks featured as favourites in this little book also contain recipes for banoffee pie: Peter Gordon's *A World in My Kitchen* and Tom Norrington Davies' *Just Like Mother Used To Make*. Do we detect a trend? Is this family favourite back in vogue?

We have also slightly modified the toffee method in the interests of speed and safety, but if you do prefer to stick to the original method, see our instructions below and follow them very carefully as we do not care to be answerable for any exploding tins. Unopened, these tins of toffee will keep indefinitely - just in case an urgent need for a really naughty (but very nice) sweet confection should arise.

Banoffee needn't be made as a pie. For a really easy breezy banoffee, layer up the ingredients nursery-trifle-style, in a ceramic or pyrex bowl or dish and serve scooped rather than sliced.

SERVES 8

FOR THE CRUST
300 g (10 oz) biscuits (cookies), crushed
we like to use gingernuts but can also endorse the use of plain or chocolate digestive or hobnobs
150 g (5 oz/1 1/4 sticks) butter, melted

FOR THE FILLING
150 g (5 oz/1 1/4) sticks butter
150 g (5 oz/2/3 cup) soft brown sugar
1 - 397 g (14 oz) tin sweetened condensed milk

2 bananas
250 ml (8 fl oz/1 cup) double (heavy) cream, chilled (easier to whip)
1 tsp instant espresso powder or finely ground coffee

MAKE THE CRUST. Mix together the biscuit crumbs and the butter and press evenly over the base and up the sides of a 24 cm (9 1/2 inch) tart tin with a removable base. Put into the fridge to firm up, about 30 minutes.

Make the filling. Heat the butter and sugar in a saucepan. When the sugar has completely dissolved, stir in the condensed milk. Bring the mixture to the boil, lower the heat and simmer, stirring constantly, until thickened and toffee coloured, about 5 minutes. Immediately pour on to the biscuit base and chill until set, about 1 1/2 hours.

Cut the bananas into 1 cm thick slices and arrange in an even layer over the toffee. Whip the cream until it holds its shape and spread in an even layer over the banana and toffee filling. Finish with a dusting of coffee. Best served chilled.

INGREDIENTS NOTE
Cooking the condensed milk still in its tin is worth doing if you are thinking of laying down some toffee for sweet tooth emergencies, so boil several at a time. Take the labels off the condensed milk tins. Place the tins in a large deep pan (with a lid), cover generously with hot water and bring to the boil. Put on the lid, adjust the heat to a steady simmer and cook for two hours, checking occasionally to make sure the tins are constantly covered with water. Keep topping up with hot water - it's vital that the water doesn't evaporate below the level of the tins or the tins will, not to put too fine a point on it, explode. Leave to cool completely before opening; this will take at least 4 hours.

THINK AHEAD
The whipped cream will stay stiff for several hours and the bananas won't turn brown if completely covered with cream.

MARILOU'S APPLE & FIVE SPICE CAKE

In an inspired moment Marilou concocted this subtly spiced cake one morning last year. It was an instant hit with customers and staff alike, so we simply had to include this new favourite in this little recipe collection. Five spice mixture is a blend of star anise, cinnamon, fennel, cloves and Sichuan pepper – and Marilou buys it across the street at The Spice Shop on Blenheim Crescent.

SERVES 8

FOR THE CAKE
100 g (3 ¹/₂ oz/³/₄ cup + 1 tbsp) plain (all-purpose) flour
2 tsp baking powder
75 g (2 ¹/₂ oz/³/₄ cup ground almonds
175 g (6 oz/1 ¹/₂ sticks) butter, softened
175 g (6 oz/⁷/₈ cup caster (granulated) sugar
1 tsp five spice mixture
salt
3 organic eggs, beaten

FOR THE TOPPING
3 apples
1 tbsp melted butter
2 tbsp sugar

HEAT THE OVEN to 180 C (350 F) Gas 4 (electric fan-assisted ovens should be set at 160 C). Butter a 24 cm (9 ¹/₂ inch) springform cake tin and line the base with baking parchment.

Sift the flour and baking powder and add the almonds. Beat the butter, sugar, five spice powder and a pinch of salt together until white and fluffy. Beat in the eggs one at a time, sprinkling in one tablespoon of the flour mix after each egg (this is to stop curdling). Gently fold in the remaining flour mix. Spread the mixture evenly over the base of the prepared tin.

Peel, quarter and core the apples. Cut each quarter into 3 slices. Arrange the apple slices slightly overlapping in concentric circles over the cake mixture. Brush the apples with melted butter and sprinkle evenly with sugar. Bake until the sides of the cake have pulled away from the tin, a skewer inserted in the middle of the cake comes out clean and the apples on top are lightly golden, about 50 minutes.

Transfer to a wire rack and leave to cool for 15 minutes. Run a knife around the sides of the cake to loosen before turning out. Serve warm or at room temperature with thick creamy yoghurt.

PEAR & FIVE SPICE CAKE
Use 3 ripe pears instead of the apples. Peel, quarter and core the pears. Cut each quarter into 3 slices. Arrange the pear slices slightly overlapping in concentric circles over the cake mixture. Finish as directed.

PLUM & FIVE SPICE CAKE
Use 4 large red plums instead of the apples. Cut the plums in quarters and arrange cut side up, skin side down over the mixture – don't push them in, just place them lightly on top because the mixture will rise as the cake bakes and you don't want the plums completely submerged in sponge. Finish as directed.

POLENTA, ALMOND & ORANGE CAKE

Gorgeously golden and drenched in sweet citrus syrup, this orange cake owes its sunny-coloured-crumb to its cornmeal content. No wheat flour's used, making this a gluten-free sweet treat and thus an extremely useful recipe to have in your culinary arsenal in these days of ever-burgeoning wheat intolerance - though do check your baking powder is labelled gluten-free before serving to coeliacs.

Stirring a teaspoonful of orange flower water into syrup before soaking perfumes this sticky, crumbly cake with a lovely floral flavour, adding, dare we say, a hint of eastern promise?!

SERVES 8

FOR THE CAKE
175 g (6 oz/1 ¹/₂ sticks) butter, softened
175 g (6 oz/³/₄ cup) caster (granulated) sugar
grated zest 3 organic oranges and 1 lemon (wash and scrub well if not organic)
juice 1 orange
250 g (8 oz/1 ³/₄ cups) polenta
125 g (4 oz/¹/₂ cup) ground almonds
2 tsp baking powder
3 organic eggs

FOR THE SYRUP
125 g (4 oz/¹/₂ cup) granulated sugar
125 ml (4 fl oz/¹/₂ cup) orange juice (about 2-3 oranges)
juice 1 lemon
1 tsp orange flower water (optional)

HEAT THE OVEN to 180 C (350 F) Gas 4 (electric fan-assisted ovens should be set to 170 C). Butter a 24 cm (9 ¹/₂ inch) springform cake tin and line the base with baking parchment.

Put the butter, sugar and orange and lemon zest in a large bowl and beat until light and fluffy. Add the orange juice, polenta, almonds, baking powder and eggs to the bowl and beat well for about 2 minutes until the cake mix is well blended. Spread the mixture evenly over the base of the prepared tin. Base until the sides of the cake have shrunk slightly away from the tin and a skewer inserted into the cake comes out clean, about 45 minutes.

Make the orange syrup. Place the sugar and orange juice in a pan over medium heat and stir until the sugar dissolves. Raise the heat, bring to the boil and simmer for 5 minutes. Remove from the heat, add the lemon juice (and orange flower water if using) and set aside to cool.

Take the cake from the oven and place on a wire rack (with a plate underneath to catch any escaping drips) but do not turn out. Straightaway pour half the cooled syrup over the hot cake and leave to stand until all the syrup has been soaked up, then pour over the remaining syrup. Run a knife round the sides of the cake to loosen, then leave to cool completely. When cold, turn out and serve with thick creamy yoghurt.

THINK AHEAD
We actually recommend baking this zestily moist cake a day ahead as it firms up and cuts neater slices when made in advance. Cool completely before storing at room temperature in an airtight container.

CHOCOLATE GINGER COOKIES

Every morning Marilou rustles up freshly baked cookies for our workshop customers to have with their coffee upstairs in the workshop kitchen above the shop. All manner of cookie recipes get road tested and every now and then a cookie is so desperately delicious that workshop attendees rush down the stairs begging the source of the recipe so as to buy up the book before we run out of copies. This recipe, so deeply and darkly chocolate-y, so sweetly studded with sticky ginger bits, proved just such an instant hit, so we thought we had better share it with you.

Our heartfelt thanks go to Mark MacDonough for bringing these almost unbearably more-ish cookies into our lives. We found the recipe in his *More Recipes from Zarbo,* the second of two deliciously eclectic books from the renowned New Zealand deli and café.

MAKES ABOUT 30 COOKIES

150 g (5 oz) dark (bittersweet) chocolate, broken into pieces
75 g (2 ¹/₂ oz/5 tbsp) butter, softened
175 g (6 oz/³/₄ cup) soft brown sugar
¹/₂ tsp natural vanilla extract
1 organic egg, beaten
115 g (3 ³/₄ oz/³/₄ cup + 3 tbsp) plain (all-purpose) flour
30 g (1 oz/5 tbsp) cocoa
1 tsp bicarbonate soda (baking soda)
salt
100 g (3 ¹/₂ oz) crystallised or stem ginger, finely chopped

HEAT THE OVEN to 100 C/220 F/Gas ¹/₄. Place the chocolate in a heatproof bowl in this very low oven and leave for 5 minutes when it should be melted; if it isn't, leave for a minute more. Stir until smooth, then leave to cool slightly. Turn up the oven to 160 C (325 F) Gas 3 (electric fan-assisted ovens should be set to 150 C). Line two baking sheets with baking parchment (or line a single sheet, but bake the cookies in batches).

Beat the butter, sugar and vanilla together until light and fluffy. Beat in the egg. Sift over the flour, cocoa, soda and a pinch of salt and add the chocolate and ginger and gently fold in until the mixture forms a sticky dough with no streaks of white or brown. Cover with cling film (plastic wrap) and chill until the dough is firm enough to handle, about 20 minutes in the freezer or 1 hour in the fridge.

Scoop out a tablespoon of the dough and roll into a ball. Place on the baking sheet and repeat with the remaining dough, leaving 4 cm (1 1/2 inches) between each ball to allow the cookies to spread. Bake until the cookies are softly set, have spread out and are slightly cracked and puffed up, 10 to 15 minutes. (If baking two baking sheets at a go, remember to swap over the oven shelves after about 8 minutes for even baking.) Leave for 5 minutes on the baking sheet to firm up slightly, then transfer to a wire rack to cool.

THINK AHEAD
These cookies are best eaten on the day of baking, but the dough itself can be made several hours ahead (even the day before) and left in the fridge until you are ready to bake.

BLANCA'S PINEAPPLE BANANA COCONUT CAKE

We are most grateful to Celia for introducing us to Blanca Valencia. She was only able to take the reins of the test kitchen for six months and she'll be back in Spain by the time this little book comes out, but she's certainly made her mark in her half-year reign. This truly fruity, lusciously moist and gently spiced cake is her special legacy.

SERVES 8

225 g (7 ¹/₂ oz/1 ³/₄ cups) plain flour
1 tsp baking powder
¹/₂ tsp bicarbonate soda (baking soda)
1 tsp ground cinnamon
1 tsp ground ginger
45 g (1 ¹/₂ oz/¹/₂ cup) desiccated coconut
450 g (15 oz) tin crushed pineapple in syrup or juice
450 g (15 oz) very ripe bananas (this can be anywhere from 2-4 bananas, depending on size)
200 g (7 oz/1 cup) light brown sugar
175 ml (6 fl oz/¹/₃ cup) sunflower oil
2 organic eggs
1 tsp natural vanilla extract

FOR THE FROSTING
30 g (1 oz/2 tbsp) butter, softened
60 g (2 oz/¹/₄ cup) mascarpone or cream cheese, softened
grated zest 1 organic lemon (wash and scrub well if not organic)
125 g (4 oz/1 cup) icing sugar
4 tbsp desiccated coconut

HEAT OVEN TO 180 C (350 F) Gas 4 (electric fan-assisted ovens should be set to 170 C). Oil a 24 cm (9 ¹/₂ inch) springform cake tin and line the base with baking parchment.

Sift the flour, baking powder, soda, cinnamon and ginger into a large mixing bowl. Stir in the coconut and mix to evenly blend, then make a well in the centre.

Drain the pineapple thoroughly over a bowl, pressing with a spoon to extract as much liquid as possible. Transfer four tablespoon of syrup or juice to another bowl with the drained crushed pineapple. Mash the bananas with a fork, add to the pineapple with the sugar, oil, eggs and vanilla, beat together thick and creamy, then pour into the well. Use a rubber spatula to fold the dry ingredients lightly but thoroughly into the wet ingredients, then pour into the prepared tin.

Bake until the sides of the cake have pulled away from the tin and a skewer inserted in the middle of the cake of the cake comes about clean, about 1 hour. Cover the cake loosely with foil during baking is it starts to overbrown. Transfer to a wire rack and leave to cool for 15 minutes. Run a knife round the sides of the cake to loosen before turning out on to the rack, then leave to cool completely.

Make the frosting. With a rubber spatula, beat the butter, mascarpone or cream cheese and lemon zest together until creamy. Sift over the icing sugar and fold into the creamy mixture until completely smooth. It's best to do this by hand as overmixing in the food processor or mixer will curdle the cheese. Spread this frosting on top of the completely cooled cake, swirling the frosting decoratively. Toast the coconut in a dry pan over a medium heat to a pale biscuit colour. Cool before sprinkling evenly over the frosting.

THINK AHEAD
This fabulously moist cake can certainly be made a day ahead; cool completely before storing at room temperature in an airtight container.

LITTLE HOT CHOCOLATE PUDDINGS

Customers are always asking for a recipe that they've had in some restaurant somewhere - a fudgy chocolate pudding that oozes gooey chocolate sauce when cut into. No one seems to know what name it goes by, with cookbook authors as well as restaurant menus differing on nomenclature – "Molten chocolate baby cakes", according to Nigella, "Melting chocolate puddings" according to Delia, but we've also come across "Little chocolate bleeding hearts" and "Soft-centred chocolate cakes". Call these scrummy puds what you will, their utter deliciousness is the one thing everyone agrees on. So we thought we'd better share our own version of this modern classic.

Our version differs from many in that we like to bury a scoop of chocolate ganache inside the chocolate pudding mixture, whereas other versions achieve their hot chocolate interiors by simply undercooking the pudding mix. We feel our marginally more labour-intensive method is well worth the effort because our soft centres do not contain raw eggs, making our puddings suitable for all the family.

SERVES 8

FOR THE HOT CHOCOLATE
75 ml (2 ¹/₂ oz/5 tbsp) double (heavy) cream
125 g (4 oz) dark (bittersweet) chocolate, broken into pieces

FOR THE PUDDINGS
200 g (7 oz/1 ¹/₂ sticks + 2 tbsp) butter
200 g (7 oz) dark (bittersweet) chocolate, broken into pieces
6 organic eggs
100 g (3 ¹/₂ oz/scant ¹/₂ cup) caster (granulated) sugar
1 tsp natural vanilla extract
60 g (2 oz/¹/₂ cup) plain flour
1 tbsp cocoa powder

HEAT THE CREAM in a small pan over a very low heat until just below simmering point and remove at once from the heat. Add the chocolate and leave to melt for a minute or so, then stir until thick and glossy. Pour into small, shallow Tupperware box and chill until set, about 3 hours – or, if you're pushed for time, pop into to the freezer for about 45 minutes.

Make the puddings. Heat the oven to 160 C (325 F) Gas 3 (electric fan-assisted ovens should be set to 150 C).

Butter eight 175 ml (6 fl oz/3/4 cup) individual pudding moulds or eight jumbo muffin pans and line the bases with rounds of baking parchment. We use silicon muffins pans and there's no need to butter or line them. If you don't already own any, we thoroughly recommend you invest: call Lakeland Plastics on 01539 488100; you'll need two pans as they come with six holes.

Melt the butter and the chocolate together, either in a microwave or in a bowl over a pan of barely simmering water, and stir until smoothly combined. Let cool slightly.

With an electric beater, whisk the eggs, sugar and vanilla until very thick, pale and mousse-like, which will take anywhere from 5 to 10 minutes.

Pour the melted chocolate mixture on to the egg mixture, then sift over the flour and cocoa. Gently but thoroughly fold in the chocolate and flour until evenly combined, with no white flour or dark chocolate streaks showing.

Divide about a third of the pudding mixture among the prepared moulds or muffin cups. Spread the mixture slightly up the sides of each mould to make an indentation. Scoop up a tablespoon of the chilled chocolate mixture, drop into the indentation in the pudding, then repeat with the other puddings. Top each mould with the remaining pudding mixture, making sure the chilled chocolate is completely sealed in, then place on a baking sheet.

Put into the oven and bake until the puddings are firm to the touch and set around the edges, 15 to 20 minutes. Cool in their moulds for 10 minute before carefully removing by running a bendy but sharp knife around the edge of each pudding (not necessary with silicon muffin tins). If you've used individual moulds, turn out directly on to the serving dish; if you've use muffin pans, turn out on to a baking sheet and then carefully transfer each pudding to the plate with a palette knife or metal spatula.

Serve the puddings without delay while hot chocolate centre is still gooey and oozes out when you break into it.

When cooking to impress, you can dress up this recipe in any number of ways. You might like to dust the puddings with a mixture of cocoa powder and icing sugar. A scattering of raspberries is lovely too, when in season. Outside raspberry season, you could serve the puddings in a pool of berry coulis – simply whiz a handful of frozen berries until smooth. Good with thick creamy yoghurt, excellent with crème fraîche, these delightful desserts are simply outstanding with vanilla ice cream – the contrast between the hot chocolate and the cold vanilla makes for a most sensuous dessert experience!

THINK AHEAD
You can make the mixture and fill the moulds several hours in advance. Place on a baking sheet, cover with cling film and put into the fridge. About a half an hour before you're ready to serve them, uncover and pop into the oven for 20 to 25 minutes (the extra 5 minutes is needed as the cakes are fridge-cold).

Left to cool, these mini cakes are nonetheless luscious as the hot chocolate interior sets to a chocolate truffle centre. You might like to warm them through with a quick blast in the microwave or 5 minutes in a hot oven.

Basics

SHORTCRUST & SWEET PASTRY

A good-tempered pastry which will line a 24 cm (9 ½) tart tin. We urge removable bases because they do make life easier when it comes to unmoulding your finished savoury or sweet tart. In fact, a great tip is to rest the tart tin on an upturned mixing bowl, and the tart will practically unmould itself as the outer metal rim just slips off.

We always recommend blind baking (pre-baking) pastry cases, whether savoury or sweet. You will need a baking sheet and some baking beans - dried beans or pasta will do just as well as the purpose-built ceramic ones. There are few things more disappointing than soggy undercooked pastry when you have gone to all the trouble of preparing a superlative tart filling, so judge the cooking time by the colour rather than by the clock and bake your pastry case until a light biscuit brown.

SHORTCRUST PASTRY

175 g (6 oz/1 ½ cups) plain (all-purpose flour) sifted
salt
90 g (3 oz/¾ stick) very cold butter, cubed
1 organic egg yolk plus 1 tbsp cold water, or 4-5 tbsp water

Lightly butter a 24 cm (9 ½ inch) tart tin and put it into the refrigerator.

Put the flour and a good pinch of salt in a food processor and aerate with a couple of quick on/off pulses. Add the butter and process till the mixture resembles fine breadcrumbs. Add the yolk and water (if necessary) and process until the pastry just draws together. Turn it out on to a lightly floured work surface and knead briefly to form a flat round.

If you don't have a food processor, do the whole thing as lightly as possible, using your fingertips to rub the butter into the flour and, when you add the liquid, pinching the whole thing into a dough.

Unless it's a very hot day, you should roll the pastry out straightaway without chilling first. Roll out to a round at least 5 cm (2 inches) larger than the tin, wrap around the rolling pin, lift into place and unroll loosely over the chilled tin. Gently lift and press the pastry into the tin to line, then roll the rolling pin over the top of the tin to trim the excess pastry. Put the pastry lined tin into the refrigerator to rest for at least an hour, or into the freezer for 15 minutes, if you're pushed for time. Do not, under any circumstances, throw the leftover pastry away, but roll it into a ball, wrap in cling film and keep at room temperature until you take your baked pastry case out of the oven (see pastry problems below).

SWEET PASTRY

Use the quantities and method given above, but mix in 45 g (1 1/2 oz/5 tbsp) sifted icing sugar with the flour and salt, and add 1/2 tsp natural vanilla extract with the egg yolk and, if necessary, water. We advise using icing sugar as its fine starchiness, as opposed to the graininess of ordinary sugar, contributes to the pastry's manageability.

BAKING BLIND (PRE-BAKING)

Put a baking sheet in the oven and heat to 190 C (375 F) Gas 5. Having a hot baking sheet in the oven helps the pastry case cook more evenly, otherwise the sides tend to cook before the base.

Line the chilled pastry case with baking parchment, fill with baking beans and cook for 10 minutes. Carefully remove the beans and paper and cook for another 10 minutes or a little longer, until a light biscuit brown.

INDIVIDUAL TARTLETS

To make six 12 cm (5 inch) shortcrust pastry cases, you will need 250 g (8 oz/2 cups) plain (all-purpose) flour, a good pinch of salt, 125 g (4 oz/1 stick) really cold butter, 2 organic egg yolks plus 2 tbsp cold water, or 7-8 tbsp cold water. Follow our instructions for making shortcrust pastry (see previous page).

To line your tins (we use fluted 12 cm (5 inch) fluted tart tins with removeable bases), arrange the tins close together on a baking sheet. Roll out the pastry until about 10 cm (4 inches) larger than all the tins bunched together. Wrap the pastry round the rolling pin and unroll gently and loosely over the tins, trying not to stretch it. Carefully lift and press the pastry into the tins, then roll the rolling pin over the tins to trim the pastry to a neat edge. Don't throw the trimmings away, but keep to patch the baked pastry in case it cracks during baking (see below). Put into the fridge or freezer to chill before blind baking (pre-baking) (see previous page).

PASTRY PROBLEMS

Having everything very cold really helps; you might like to put your butter cubes in the freezer for 5 minutes extra chilling to keep everything nice and cold, while some people keep their flour in the freezer both for pastry purposes and because it keeps better.

If your pastry is too crumbly, roll it out between two pieces of cling film (plastic wrap). If it is too soft because the ingredients are too warm, or you have added too much liquid, chill it first, until firm but not rock-hard, before rolling out in between cling film. Cling film, as you can see, is but a little short of a universal panacea, working wonders with all kinds of pastry problems.

Well, you lined the tin, rested the pastry and baked it blind. Hopefully you now have a perfect pastry case before you. If, however, you find you have a less than perfect pastry case with one or two or lots of little cracks in it (evil little cracks though which the tart filling threatens to seep), do not despair. This is where your leftover pastry will come to the rescue. Gently press scraps of the leftover raw pastry to the cracks in the hot pastry shell and the heat will stick the raw and the cooked pastry together and seal up the cracks. Easy as pie.

Menus

THE ENCYCLOPEDIA of
FOOD

1500 INGREDIENTS AND HOW TO COOK THEM

THE ENCYCLOPEDIA FOOD

DO-AHEAD DINNER

Egyptian Feta Salad with Dill & Mint
(see page 62)

Braised Lamb with Tamarind & Dates
(see page 56)
Buttered Couscous

Polenta, Almond & Orange Cake
(see page 94)
Thick creamy yoghurt

VEGETARIAN CELEBRATION MEAL

Saffron, Tahini & Yoghurt Soup
(see page 24)

Aubergines with Spiced Walnut Sauce
(see page 38)
Red Pepper Bulgur
(see page 72)
Green leaf salad dressed with lemon and olive oil

Red Wine & Chocolate Cake
(see page 86)

DINNER IN A DASH

Courgette, Goat Cheese & Basil Soup
(see page 18)

Spicy Sausage Pasta with Capers, Olives & Feta
(see page 50)

Chocolate Ginger Cookies
(see page 96)

A WINTER WARMER

Roast Pumpkin, Garlic & Rosemary Soup with Feta
(see page 13)

Maghrebi Meatballs with Spinach & Chickpeas
(see page 32)

Cinnamon Swirl Sour Cream Cake
(see page 88)
Best vanilla ice cream

LIGHT LUNCH FOR FRIENDS

Spicy Sausage & Bean Soup with Roast Tomatoes
(see page 10)

Ricotta Gnocchi with Basil
(see page 31)
Green leaf salad dressed with lemon and olive oil

Plum, Lemon & Coconut Cake
(see page 78)

DRESS-UP DINNER

Roast Sweet Potato Soup with Thai Flavours
(see page 23)

Crab, Chilli & Lime Scattered Sushi
(see page 54)

Spiced Crisp Roast Pork Belly with Caramelised Peanut & Chilli Relish
(see page 46)
Crisp Salad with Chilli Lime Dressing
(see page 69)

Little Hot Chocolate Puddings
(see page 100)
Best vanilla ice cream

TABLE OF EQUIVALENTS

LIQUIDS CONVERSIONS

Metric	Imperial	US
30 ml	1 fl oz	2 tbsp
45 ml	1 1/2 fl oz	3 tbsp
60 ml	2 fl oz	1/4 cup
75 ml	2 1/2 fl oz	1/3 cup
90 ml	3 fl oz	1/3 cup + 1 tbsp
100 ml	3 1/2 fl oz	1/3 cup + 2 tbsp
125 ml	4 fl oz	1/2 cup
150 ml	5 fl oz	2/3 cup
175 ml	6 fl oz	3/4 cup
200 ml	7 fl oz	3/4 cup + 2 tbsp
250 ml	8 fl oz	1 cup
275 ml	9 fl oz	1 cup + 2 tbsp
300 ml	10 fl oz	1 1/4 cups
325 ml	11 fl oz	1 1/3 cups
350 ml	12 fl oz	1 1/2 cups
375 ml	13 fl oz	1 2/3 cups
400 ml	14 fl oz	1 3/4 cups
450 ml	15 fl oz	1 3/4 cups +2 tbsp
500 ml	16 fl oz	1 pint (2 cups)
600 ml	1 pint	2 1/2 cups
900 ml	1 1/2 pint	3 3/4 cups
1 litre	1 3/4 pints	4 cups

OVEN TEMPERATURES

Celsius	Fahrenheit	Gas
120	250	1/2
140	275	1
150	300	2
160	325	3
180	350	4
190	375	5
200	400	6
220	425	7
230	450	8
240	475	9
260	500	10

Note: Reduce the temperature by 20 C (68 F) for fan-assisted ovens

USEFUL EQUIVALENTS

Flour
1 cup	4 oz

Cocoa
1 cup	3 oz

Flaked Almonds
1 cup	3 oz

Ground Almonds
1 cup	3 3/4 oz

Chopped Nuts
1 cup	4 oz

White Sugar
1 cup	7 oz

Brown Sugar
1 cup	8 oz

Icing Sugar
1 cup	4 oz

WEIGHT CONVERSIONS

Metric	UK/US
15 g	1/2 oz
30 g	1 oz
45 g	1 1/2 oz
60 g	2 oz
75 g	2 1/2 oz
90 g	3 oz
100 g	3 1/2 oz
125 g	4 oz
150 g	5 oz
175 g	6 oz
200 g	7 oz
250 g	8 oz
275 g	9 oz
300 g	10 oz
325 g	11 oz
350 g	12 oz
375 g	13 oz
400 g	14 oz
450 g	15 oz
500 g	1 lb

PLEASE NOTE: A few golden rules of measuring: always stick religiously to one system, never mix and match. When measuring liquids, place the jug on a flat surface, bend down and check for accuracy at eye level. When using cups, spoon the ingredient into the cup, mounding slightly, and level off with the back of a knife. Do not use the cup as a scoop or tap the cup on the work surface. Bear in mind that these tables are approximate; they do not completely conform to the official conversions, but we have found them useful.

RECIPE LIST

SOUPS

Spicy Sausage & Bean Soup with Roast Tomatoes	10
Ham Hock & Split Pea Soup	12
Roast Pumpkin, Garlic & Rosemary Soup with Feta	13
Farro & Borlotti Soup	14
Barley & Borlotti Soup	15
Tomato & Tamarind Soup with Toasted Spices	16
Courgette, Goat Cheese & Basil Soup	18
Lentil & Chorizo Soup	19
Fennel Soup with Orange Gremolata	20
All-Season Pappa al Pommodoro	22
Roast Sweet Potato Soup with Thai Flavours	23
Saffron, Tahini & Yoghurt Soup	24
Chicken & Roast Pepper Soup with Basil	25

MAIN COURSES

Smoked Haddock, Leek & Potato Pie	28
Ricotta Gnocchi with Gorgonzola Sauce	30
Ricotta Gnocchi with Basil	31
Maghrebi Meatballs with Spinach & Chickpeas	32
Pasta with Porcini Chicken Sauce	34
Aromatic Pork Belly Hot Pot	36
Aubergines with Spiced Walnut Sauce	38
Spicy Braised Oxtail	40
Coriander Chilli Fish Curry	43
Poached Chicken with Sweet Soy	44
Spiced Crisp Roast Pork Belly with Caramelised Peanut & Chilli Relish	46
Cumin Lamb & Aubergine Stew	48
Spicy Sausage Pasta with Capers, Olives & Feta	50
Catalan Chicken with Prawns & Picada	52
Crab, Chilli & Lime Scattered Sushi	54
Braised Lamb with Tamarind & Dates	56
Filo Spinach & Sausage Pie	58
Cardamom Yoghurt Chicken	60

SALADS & SIDES

SWEET THINGS

BASICS